# Pages to Profit

*How to Turn Your Book into Clients, Cash, and Credibility*

Book One

## Michael O'Connor

*Ardith*

The freedom to publish

Ardith Publishing

Library and Archives Canada Cataloguing in Publication

CIP data on file with the National Library and Archives

ISBN (trade paperback) 978-1-55483-590-4
ISBN (ebook) 978-1-55483-591-1

Ardith Publishing
520 Princess Ave.
London, Ontario, Canada
N6B 2B8

*www. ardithpublishing.com*

for Linda

A free gift for you.

## Write & Publish Your Book in Just 3 Days — With the Help of AI!

Ever dreamed of writing a book but felt overwhelmed by the process? *3 Days to Book* is your fast-track guide to planning, writing, and publishing a professional book in just 72 hours—no prior experience needed. This free resource reveals how to harness the power of AI tools like ChatGPT, Jasper, and Canva to go from blank page to published with ease. Whether you're a coach, entrepreneur, or expert with a message to share, this guide helps you skip the struggle and start your author journey with confidence.

Inside, you'll get a step-by-step blueprint, AI-powered writing and formatting hacks, marketing tips, and even a 10% discount on publishing services with Ardith Publishing. Plus, when you download the guide, you'll receive helpful emails filled with expert advice, publishing insights, and exclusive deals to support your success every step of the way. Don't wait—your bestselling book is just three days away.

www.3-day-aiforpagetoprofits.getresponsesite.com

# Contents

# Introduction

Books have always been my compass. They've shaped my thoughts, challenged my assumptions, and opened doors to worlds I never knew existed. Some books lit a fire inside me, others held up a mirror, forcing me to see myself clearly for the first time. But the most powerful ones? They didn't just teach me something new—they changed the way I saw what was possible.

From an early age, I knew stories held power. Not just the ones bound in paper and ink, but the ones we live, the ones we tell, the ones that define us. A book isn't just a collection of words; it's a bridge—to new ideas, to new opportunities, to new identities. That belief became the foundation of my life's work.

I built Ardith Publishing on that same conviction: that books are more than just products—they are tools for transformation. For independent authors and business professionals alike, a book is not just a personal milestone; it's a gateway to influence, credibility, and impact. And yet, so many talented, insightful people hesitate to take that step. They doubt their story, their expertise, their voice. My job is to help them see what I've always known: that their story matters, and that the world is waiting to hear it.

I've seen firsthand how a well-crafted book can open doors that seemed permanently shut. It can position a business leader as an industry authority. It can establish an entrepreneur as a go-to expert. It can turn a personal journey into a movement. Whether you're looking to grow a brand, attract opportunities, or leave a legacy, your book is more than a tool—it's a statement. And when done right, it's a force.

That's why I wrote this book. To pull back the curtain, to demystify the process, to show you that publishing isn't just for the select few—it's for you. Whether you're an aspiring author, a business owner, or a thought leader with something to say, this book will guide you through the steps of writing, publishing, and leveraging your book for maximum impact. It's about more than just getting your name on a cover—it's about making sure your book works for you, long after the last page is turned.

I won't just tell you what to do—I'll show you how it's done. You'll find practical strategies, real-world examples, and a roadmap to navigate the publishing world with confidence. No fluff, no vague advice—just the tools and insights you need to write the book that will take your career, your brand, and your influence to the next level.

Because your story matters. Your expertise matters. And if you're ready to take that next step, I'm here to make sure your book doesn't just exist—it thrives. Let's get started.

# Chapter 1
## Your Book as a Business Catalyst

In the bustling world of entrepreneurship and rapid business growth, one tool stands out as a genuine game-changer: the published book. A book goes far beyond words on pages; it can become a powerful business catalyst that propels a career to new heights. Whether you're a solopreneur carving out a space in a crowded marketplace or an established business owner aiming to expand your empire, writing a book can reshape your professional landscape in unimaginable ways.

Think about it—while the marketplace is full of voices trying to be heard, an author's voice is distinct. It cuts through the noise with a message of authority and expertise. As a result, your book doesn't merely add credibility; it acts as a tool, a beacon that attracts clients, opportunities, and recognition.

### The Metamorphosis: From Business Owner to Author

Imagine this scene: you walk into a high-stakes meeting. The room falls silent, and all eyes turn to you. But you're not just another face among business owners. You're an author. The atmosphere shifts as you take your seat. In that moment, you've transcended the role of a business owner or consultant and stepped into the world of an authority figure. This is the transformative magic of authorship.

Authorship represents more than a title; it's a new level of recognition. When you write a book, you're not just sharing your thoughts or insights. You're making a powerful statement: "I know this subject deeply. So deeply, in fact, that I've written the book on it." And that's something people respect and remember.

### Real-World Example: Tony Robbins' Success Story

Think about Tony Robbins, who transitioned from a life coach to an international motivational powerhouse. His book *Unlimited Power* was not just a publication; it was the tool that elevated him from the realm of one-on-one coaching to a global stage. His words didn't just reach clients—they reached audiences worldwide, connecting deeply with people he'd never even met. Writing transformed his image, and today, Robbins is recognized as a leader in personal development, his book an enduring testament to his expertise and approach.

This is the power of authorship. A well-written book doesn't merely educate; it captivates, inspires, and positions you as the leader in your field. When you write a book, you're sharing knowledge, but you're also building a bridge to opportunities that may have seemed beyond reach.

### The Author's Aura: A Perception Revolution

The moment your book appears on a shelf, a remarkable transformation occurs. People view you differently. You're no longer just knowledgeable about your field; you become a thought leader, an innovator, and a voice people seek. This shift in perception is subtle yet profound, impacting nearly every aspect of your professional life.

Consider the authors you admire in your industry. Their words resonate in a way that few others do. Their advice feels insightful, almost visionary. Why? Because they've demonstrated a commitment to their craft by distilling their knowledge into a book. It's not just expertise; it's a marker of authority.

## Case in Point: Brené Brown and Daring Greatly

Look at Brené Brown, who turned her book *Daring Greatly* into a touchstone for conversations about vulnerability and courage. She didn't simply write a book; she started a movement that influenced leaders, organizations, and individuals worldwide. Her readers know her words carry weight, not just because of her expertise but because she invested time, thought, and dedication into sharing her message in book form. Brown's book solidified her place as an authority in her field.

By writing a book, you can join these ranks. Your book is not merely pages bound together. It becomes a supercharged business card, an indelible credibility booster. Unlike traditional marketing materials that may quickly fade from memory, a book claims prime real estate on desks, bookshelves, and digital libraries. Each glance etches your expertise further into the reader's mind, cementing your status as the go-to source in your industry.

## Passion vs. Purpose: Writing with Intent

Many aspiring authors dream of pouring their

hearts onto the page, creating a work of unbridled passion. But in the business world, passion alone often isn't enough. Purpose, on the other hand, drives success. Writing a book with clear business objectives is fundamentally different from writing simply to share one's story. It's about strategically crafting a narrative that not only showcases your expertise but also attracts opportunities.

Take Simon Sinek, whose book *Start with Why* wasn't just a philosophical exploration of purpose-driven business—it was his platform. Sinek's message resonated deeply, making him a go-to consultant for business leaders around the globe. His book transformed him into a thought leader. For Sinek, his book was more than an outlet for passion; it was a strategic business asset that built his brand, opened doors to speaking engagements, and amplified his voice.

To write a book that aligns with your business goals, start by knowing your audience. What are their pain points? What solutions do they desperately need? How can your unique expertise address their challenges? Writing with these questions in mind bridges your audience's needs with your business objectives.

Writing with intent doesn't mean sacrificing authenticity. On the contrary, it's about channeling your passion to serve your readers and your business. It's about finding that sweet spot where your expertise, your readers' needs, and your professional goals intersect.

## Your Book: A Modern Business Growth Engine

In today's digital landscape, anyone can claim expertise with a polished website or active social media presence. Yet, a book remains a powerful way to differentiate yourself. A book has staying power. It's a physical or digital testament to your knowledge and authority, standing strong amidst the shifting sands of online content.

Think of your book as a Swiss Army knife for business growth. Here's why:

1. **Establishes Credibility** – Becoming an author elevates your professional status instantly. It's a public declaration that you've dedicated time, effort, and thought to your field.

2. **Attracts High-Value Clients** – A book acts as a powerful lead magnet, drawing in clients who are genuinely interested in your expertise.

3. **Opens Doors to Media Opportunities** – Journalists, podcast hosts, and bloggers constantly seek expert voices. Your book gives them a compelling reason to reach out to you.

4. **Secures Speaking Engagements** – Event organizers prioritize authors for speaking roles, as your book acts as proof of your knowledge and your ability to engage audiences.

5. **Expands Your Network** – Writing a book often involves reaching out to experts for quotes, case studies, or even forewords. This process naturally expands your professional network.

**6. Generates Passive Income** – Although not the primary goal for most business authors, book sales can create a steady income stream.

**7. Provides Content for Other Platforms** – Your book can be repurposed into blog posts, social media updates, podcasts, and more, fueling your content marketing.

### Real-World Example: Jen Sincero and You Are a Badass

Jen Sincero's book *You Are a Badass* began as a way to help readers find confidence and achieve their goals. But it became much more—it became a brand, an empire that allowed her to expand into workshops, coaching, and a follow-up series. Her book didn't just attract readers; it pulled in followers, fans, and opportunities to connect. Her book is still selling, still reaching new people, and still doing the heavy lifting for her brand.

Your book, too, can become a tireless ambassador, working around the clock to establish your authority and elevate your brand. It's an investment that continues to pay off by building credibility, reaching clients, and opening new doors.

### Maximizing Your Literary Asset

Many first-time authors make the rookie mistake of publishing their book and waiting for success to come to them. But a book isn't a golden ticket—it's a powerful tool that requires strategic use. To fully harness its potential, think of your book as an integral part of your business strategy.

Here's how to maximize the impact of your book:

## Practical Applications

**1. Client Acquisition** – Send signed copies to new clients as part of their onboarding process. It adds a personal touch and reinforces your expertise from day one.

**2. Speaking Engagements** – When pitching yourself as a speaker, include a copy of your book with your proposal. It demonstrates your knowledge and significantly increases your chances of being selected.

**3. Lead Generation** – Offer chapters or excerpts as lead magnets on your website. These free downloads in exchange for email addresses allow you to build a contact list of potential clients already interested in your expertise.

**4. Content Marketing** – Repurpose sections of your book as blog posts, social media updates, podcast episodes, or video content. Your book provides a wealth of material that can fuel your content marketing efforts.

**5. Networking Tool** – Use your book as a memorable gift when meeting potential partners or influential people in your industry. It's far more impactful than a business card.

**6. Media Kit** – Include your book in your media kit

when reaching out to journalists or applying for speaking roles. A book gives weight to your credentials and serves as tangible proof of your expertise.

7. **Workshop Material** – Use your book as the foundation for workshops or online courses, creating new revenue streams and positioning you as an educator in your field.

By strategically integrating these practices, you ensure that your book isn't just a title; it's an active, influential component of your business.

## The Journey Begins: From Idea to Published Author

Understanding the potential of a book is the first step. The next is learning how to bring your book to life. From the spark of an idea to a published work, the process of writing a book involves multiple stages

## The Process

1. **Idea Refinement** – Start by honing your book idea. Ensure it aligns with your business goals and addresses a genuine need in your industry.

2. **Outline Development** – Structure your ideas into a comprehensive outline, making sure there's a logical flow and progression in your content.

3. **Writing Support** – Whether you're drafting independently or collaborating with a writing coach, focus on clarity, consistency, and compelling communication.

**4. Editing and Proofreading** – A professional editor can polish your manuscript to meet high standards of quality, refining everything from grammar to overall structure.

**5. Design and Layout** – Create a cover that captures your brand and an interior layout that's professional and visually appealing.

**6. Publishing** – Navigating the publishing process, from ISBN registration to distribution setup, is essential for bringing your book to the world.

**7. Marketing and Promotion** – Even the best books need promotion. Leverage social media, email marketing, book events, and partnerships to reach your target audience effectively.

Remember, this process is not just about producing a book; it's about creating a powerful asset that aligns with your business and resonates with your audience.

### Your Next Chapter Starts Now

Writing a book isn't only about becoming an author. It's about cementing your role as the go-to expert in your field, crafting a brand that resonates more than any business card. Whether you're aiming to expand your client base, secure speaking engagements, or break into new industries, a book is the ultimate business investment.

The journey to becoming a published author is both thrilling and transformative. Your story matters, and by sharing it, you create a lasting impact that goes beyond words on a page. In a world that values expertise, a book is a beacon. It is proof of your authority, a testament to your knowledge, and an open door to endless possibilities.

The world awaits your voice, your expertise, and your insight. And right now, all that's missing is your book. Let this be the beginning of a journey that elevates your business, strengthens your brand, and solidifies your legacy.

Write your way to success and make your mark.

# Chapter 2

## Establishing Credibility and Expertise - Your Book as a Beacon of Authority

In the crowded world of professional services, a book is like a lighthouse. It signals your expertise, guiding clients to your unique approach. Writing a book does more than fill pages—it fills a gap in your professional identity. It transforms you from one of many to *the one* who stands out.

Picture this: you enter a room filled with industry peers. You're not just another face in the crowd. You're an author. The air shifts. Eyes turn. Curiosity piques. That's the unmistakable power of authorship.

### The Alchemy of Authorship: Turning Knowledge into Gold

Once your book hits the shelves, a magical transformation occurs. You shed the image of an ordinary professional and emerge as an authority. This change isn't only perception—it's a tangible shift in how people interact with you.

Your book becomes a silent ambassador. It speaks volumes about your expertise when you're not in the room. It opens doors that were previously closed, and it whispers your worth into the ears of potential clients before you even shake their hands. But why does this happen? What is it about authorship that makes it such a potent catalyst for credibility?

## Real-World Example: Ramit Sethi and I Will Teach You to Be Rich

Ramit Sethi, author of *I Will Teach You to Be Rich*, wrote his book to guide readers in managing personal finances effectively. But he didn't stop there. Ramit used his book as a launchpad to build a financial empire, including an online business, courses, and a consulting firm. His book has been reprinted multiple times and continues to draw clients to his programs. His authority in finance wasn't just established through the content itself, but through the credibility his book brought him.

The effect is clear: a well-written book does more than educate. It opens doors to new business opportunities, helps build your reputation, and establishes you as a recognized leader.

## The Psychology Behind Author Credibility

Humans are wired to respect the written word. For centuries, books have been viewed as sources of knowledge, wisdom, and authority. When someone takes the time to compile their knowledge into a book, we instinctively assign them a higher status. If they wrote a book, we think, they must know what they're talking about.

This psychological effect plays out in boardrooms and business deals every day. Imagine two consultants competing for the same project. Their skills are comparable. Their experience is similar. But one has written a book on the subject. Who do you think wins the contract?

The author wins. Every time. Not necessarily because they're better, but because they've leveraged the power of authorship to tip the scales in their favour.

## Case Study: Marcus Sheridan and They Ask, You Answer

Marcus Sheridan was an ordinary pool salesman. Then he wrote *They Ask, You Answer*, a book addressing common customer questions and concerns. This book didn't just build credibility—it launched Sheridan into the realm of business consulting. His book became a go-to guide for marketing professionals and business owners looking to answer client questions proactively. Sheridan's experience highlights the psychology behind authorship: when he published, he transformed his everyday experience into expert-level insight.

By writing a book, Sheridan didn't only improve his credibility—he built a new career as an authority in his field.

## Standing Out in a Sea of Sameness

In today's digital age, everyone's shouting for attention. Social media feeds are overflowing, inboxes are flooded, and websites often blur together. But a book? A book cuts through the noise like a foghorn on a quiet night.

Writing a book is the ultimate differentiator. It sets you apart in ways that other marketing tools cannot match. Here's why:

1. **Depth of Knowledge**: Anyone can write a blog post or share a tweet, but only a few can write a comprehensive book. Authorship demonstrates a depth of knowledge that's hard to fake.

2. **Commitment to Craft**: Writing a book requires time, effort, and dedication. It shows you're serious about your field.

3. **Tangible Expertise**: A book is a physical or digital manifestation of your expertise. It's something clients can hold, read, and refer to over time.

4. **Lasting Impact**: Social media posts may fade into obscurity, but a book endures. It continues to work for you long after it's published.

Your competitors might have sleek websites or impressive social media followings, but adding "author" to your credentials elevates you to an entirely different level.

### The Client's Perspective: Why Authors Win

Put yourself in your client's shoes. They need someone to solve a pressing issue. They have options, lots of them. How do they decide who to hire?

They look for signals of expertise. And nothing signals expertise quite like authorship. Here's what goes through a client's mind when they see that you've written a book:

**Trust**: "If they took the time to write a book, they must really know their stuff."

**Authority**: "They're not just practicing their craft—they're defining it."

**Dedication**: "Writing a book takes serious commitment. They must be passionate about this field."

**Problem-Solving Ability**: "If they can break down complex ideas into a book, they can probably solve my problem, too."

This shift in perception is invaluable. It takes you from being one of many potential hires to standing out as the obvious choice.

### Real-World Example: Tim Ferriss and The 4-Hour Workweek

Tim Ferriss had been testing unconventional productivity and lifestyle approaches for years. But his book, *The 4-Hour Workweek*, did more than capture his techniques—it revolutionized the way people think about work and lifestyle. Readers flocked to Ferriss not just because his ideas were new, but because his book gave him authority. Since its publication, Ferriss has built a massive following, a podcast, and even more books. The book wasn't just a project; it was the foundation for his entire career.

### Choosing Your Book's North Star: Aligning Topic with Expertise

Now that you understand the power of authorship, the next step is crucial: choosing your topic. This isn't just about writing what you know; it's about choosing a topic that will position you precisely where you want to be.

Your book's topic is like your professional North

Star. It guides your career trajectory, attracts the right clients, and opens the right doors. Choose wisely.

## Framework for Choosing Your Book's Topic

**1. Expertise Audit**: Identify what you know better than anyone else. What problems have you solved repeatedly for clients? List your areas of deep expertise.

**2. Client Pain Points**: What issues keep your ideal clients up at night? What are the most common questions they ask you? Look for the intersection between their needs and your knowledge.

**3. Future Positioning**: Where do you want to be in five years? Your book should bridge the gap between where you are now and where you want to go.

**4. Market Gap Analysis**: What's missing in your industry's literature? Is there a fresh perspective you can offer? Filling a gap can set you apart as an innovator.

**5. Passion Check**: Which topics energize you? What could you discuss for hours without getting bored? Passion fuels perseverance, especially in the writing process.

Remember, a focused book packs more punch than a broad one. Don't try to cover everything. Choose a specific problem and solve it thoroughly.

## Leveraging Your Book: From Pages to Profits

Your book isn't just a product—it's a versatile business tool. Here's how to leverage it for maximum impact:

1. **The Ultimate Business Card**: Hand out your book in place of a traditional business card. It's memorable, valuable, and shows your expertise in a way no card can.

2. **Client Onboarding Tool**: Give new clients a copy of your book. It sets the tone for your working relationship and gives them a deeper understanding of your approach.

3. **Speaking Engagement Magnet**: Event organizers love booking authors. A book opens doors to speaking opportunities you might not otherwise access.

4. **Media Magnet**: Journalists and podcast hosts constantly look for expert voices. Your book positions you as a go-to source in your field.

5. **Content Goldmine**: Repurpose your book content into articles, blog posts, and social media posts. It's a deep well of material for all your marketing.

6. **Partnership Catalyst**: Potential partners and collaborators take authors seriously. Your book can attract other experts in your industry, amplifying your reach.

**7. Workshop and Course Material**: Use your book as the foundation for workshops, online courses, or consulting packages. It can serve as the backbone for a suite of products.

A book's value isn't measured in sales alone. Its real worth lies in the opportunities it creates and the doors it opens.

### Example of Leveraging Authorship: Michael Hyatt and Platform

Michael Hyatt, former CEO of Thomas Nelson Publishers, used his book *Platform: Get Noticed in a Noisy World* as the launchpad for a thriving business. The book was just the beginning. He used it to create online courses, host a popular podcast, offer coaching programs, and even release software. Hyatt didn't view his book as a standalone product; he saw it as a tool for building a business ecosystem around his ideas.

### The Art of Authority: Weaving Stories into Your Expertise

Facts inform, but stories transform. Your book shouldn't just be a straightforward recital of knowledge. It should be a collection of stories that bring your expertise to life.

Stories are powerful for several reasons:

**1. Emotional Connection**: Stories engage emotions, making your content memorable.

**2. Real-World Application**: They show your ideas in action.

**3. Trust Building**: Sharing experiences builds trust with readers.

**4. Simplification**: Stories make complex concepts easy to understand.

**How to Weave Stories Into Your Book:**

**1. Personal Anecdotes**: Share your journey and the lessons you've learned along the way.

**2. Client Case Studies**: Show real-world examples of problems you've solved (with permission, of course).

**3. Hypothetical Scenarios**: Illustrate concepts with *what if* scenarios to make them relatable.

**4. Historical Examples**: Tie in relevant historical events to add depth.

**5. Metaphors and Analogies**: Use comparisons to clarify complex ideas.

In writing, you're not just sharing information—you're crafting a narrative that positions you as the trusted guide on your reader's journey.

## From Author to Authority: Your Next Steps

Writing a book is your ticket to the upper echelons of your industry. It's a transformative process that can turn expertise into authority. But knowledge without action achieves little.

Here's your roadmap to success:

1. **Define Your Topic**: Use the framework to choose the topic that aligns with your goals.

2. **Outline Your Book**: Map out the structure. Decide which key points you'll cover and in what order.

3. **Set a Writing Schedule**: Consistency is essential. Dedicate time to write regularly.

4. **Gather Stories**: Start collecting anecdotes, case studies, and relevant examples.

5. **Build Your Platform**: Start talking about your book now. Build anticipation and lay the groundwork for its release.

Remember, your book is more than a collection of pages—it's a beacon of your expertise, a testament to your knowledge, and a tool for building your future.

Take the first step today and begin crafting a book that not only establishes your credibility but also opens the door to countless new possibilities. Write your way to influence, opportunity, and an unshakable legacy.

# Chapter 3

## Expanding Your Professional Network - Your Book as a Bridge to New Opportunities

Imagine holding a key that unlocks doors you never knew existed. That key is your book. It's more than words on pages—it's a passport to a world of connections, collaborations, and opportunities. From the moment your book hits the shelves, you possess a powerful tool that magnetizes industry leaders, influencers, and potential clients to you.

Networking has always been the lifeblood of business success. But add a book to the mix, and you're playing a whole new game. You're no longer just another face in the crowd, vying for attention. You're an author, offering tangible value upfront—your expertise, your insights, your unique perspective, all neatly packaged between two covers. This is how you transform networking from a necessary chore into an exhilarating journey of connection and growth.

### Your Book: The Ultimate Conversation Starter

Picture this: You're at a crowded industry event. The room buzzes with chatter, business cards exchange hands like rapid-fire, and elevator pitches float through the air. How do you stand out? Simple.

You reach into your bag and pull out your book.

Instantly, the dynamic shifts. You're not just another professional with a business card—you're an author with a message. Your book becomes a bridge, spanning the gap between you and potential connections. It's a tangible representation of your expertise, a conversation piece that opens doors to meaningful dialogues.

But don't just hand over your book and walk away. Use it as a launchpad for deeper connections. After a brief introduction, you might say, "I'd love to give you a copy of my book. It dives deep into the challenges we were just discussing. I think you'll find some interesting insights that could benefit your work."

People will remember you. Not just because you gave them a book, but because you offered them value. You stood out in the sea of faces by sharing your expertise in a tangible, memorable way.

Here's a pro tip: Always carry a few copies of your book to industry events. You never know when you'll meet someone who could become a valuable connection. Your book allows you to turn any chance encounter into a memorable interaction.

### Crafting a Book Launch that Catapults Your Network

Your book launch isn't just a celebration—it's a golden opportunity to exponentially expand your professional network. A well-orchestrated book launch can be the catalyst that propels your career to new heights, bringing together influencers, thought leaders, and potential collaborators who are genuinely interested in what you have to say.

But how do you transform your launch from a simple signing event into a networking powerhouse? It starts with strategic planning.

First, think carefully about your guest list. Who are the movers and shakers in your industry? Which influencers align with your book's message? Don't rely on mass invitations or impersonal social media blasts. Take the time to reach out individually to key figures. A personal invitation can work wonders in getting the right people in the room.

Next, consider the format of your launch. A simple signing might not be enough to spark meaningful connections. Instead, why not organize a panel discussion or workshop centered around the themes of your book? This approach provides value to attendees, giving them a compelling reason to engage more deeply with you and your ideas.

For example, if your book is about innovative marketing strategies, you could host a panel discussion with other marketing experts, discussing the future of the industry. This not only showcases your expertise but also positions you as a convener of important conversations in your field.

Remember, the more value you provide at your launch, the more likely people are to remember you and stay in touch. Your book launch isn't just about you—it's about creating an experience that benefits everyone who attends.

### Taking Your Book on the Road: A Journey of Connections

Why limit yourself to a single launch event when you can take your book—and your networking opportunities—on the road? A book tour, whether virtual or in-person, is a powerful way to tap into new markets and meet people outside your immediate circle.

Each stop on your tour is a fresh opportunity to connect with new influencers, potential clients, and business leaders who could help expand your network. But don't just show up and read from your book. Make each event unique and valuable for attendees.

For instance, you could partner with local businesses or organizations that align with your book's themes. If your book is about sustainable business practices, team up with a local eco-friendly company for your event. This not only provides an interesting venue but also introduces you to a whole new network of like-minded professionals.

Virtual tours can be equally effective. Host online workshops, webinars, or Q&A sessions based on your book's content. The digital format allows you to connect with people from all over the world, vastly expanding your potential network.

Remember, the goal of your book tour isn't just to sell books—it's to build relationships. Follow up with the connections you make at each stop. A simple email saying how much you enjoyed meeting them can be the start of a valuable professional relationship.

### Collaborating with Influencers: Your Book as a Bridge

Your book isn't just a product—it's a platform for collaboration with influencers and thought leaders in your industry. These collaborations can have a lasting impact on your career, opening doors to new audiences and opportunities.

Start by identifying influencers whose work aligns with the themes of your book. These are individuals whose audiences would benefit from your message, and who might be interested in what you have to say. But don't just send them your book out of the blue. Craft a personalized message explaining why you think your book would resonate with them and their audience.

Once you've made that initial connection, look for opportunities to collaborate. You could invite an influencer to write a foreword for your book or contribute a guest chapter. Alternatively, offer to appear on their podcast or co-host a live event that promotes both your book and their platform.

These partnerships do more than just expand your reach—they establish your credibility by association. When an respected influencer in your field endorses your work, it sends a powerful message to their audience about your expertise.

Take a leaf out of Ryan Holiday's books. His work, *The Obstacle Is the Way* caught the attention of high-profile figures, including sports teams, business leaders, and elite athletes. Holiday didn't just write a book—he created a philosophy that resonated with influential figures. This led to collaborations that dramatically expanded his professional network and cemented his status as a thought leader.

The lesson here is clear: view your book as a networking tool, not just a product. By proactively reaching out to influencers and seeking collaborations, you can significantly expand your professional reach and open doors to opportunities you might never have imagined.

## Case Study: Ryan Holiday's Network Expansion Through The Obstacle Is the Way

Ryan Holiday's journey with *The Obstacle Is the Way* is a masterclass in using a book to expand your professional network. Holiday didn't just write a book for the general public—he crafted a message that resonated deeply with a specific audience. His focus on stoicism and overcoming challenges struck a chord with elite athletes, sports teams, and high-powered business leaders who saw their own struggles reflected in the principles he discussed.

But Holiday didn't stop at writing the book. He leveraged it to build relationships with these influential figures. His book became a key that unlocked doors to conversations with NFL quarterbacks, NBA coaches, and Fortune 500 CEOs. As a result, Holiday's network expanded far beyond the literary world, encompassing sports, business, and beyond.

This networking wasn't accidental—it was intentional. Holiday wrote with a specific audience in mind and actively reached out to those who aligned with his message. His book became a bridge to relationships that would have been difficult, if not impossible, to forge otherwise.

The takeaway is clear: when you write a book that resonates with a particular group, you can use it to connect with influencers in that space. The opportunities that follow may be more significant than anything you could have imagined when you first sat down to write.

## Hosting a Targeted Book Launch: Your Networking Powerhouse

Let's get practical. How can you make your book launch a networking powerhouse? Here's a step-by-step strategy:

1. **Curate Your Guest List:** Make a list of industry influencers and thought leaders who align with your book's themes. Don't just invite everyone you know. Be strategic. Think about who you want to connect with and why.

2. **Personalize Your Invitations**: Send personalized invitations to your key targets. Explain why their presence would be meaningful and what value they'll gain from attending. Make them feel special and important.

3. **Create a Valuable Event Format**: Instead of a simple book signing, host a panel discussion or a roundtable on a topic related to your book. Invite a few key influencers to participate. This not only brings value to attendees but also puts you in direct collaboration with those influencers.

4. **Prepare Thoughtful Introductions**: Research your guests beforehand. Prepare thoughtful introductions that can spark meaningful conversations. Show that you've done your homework and are genuinely interested in connecting.

5. **Provide Exclusive Content**: Offer something ex-

clusive to attendees. This could be a special edition of your book, a supplementary workbook, or access to a private online community. Give them a reason to engage beyond the event itself.

6. **Facilitate Connections**: Don't just focus on your own networking. Look for opportunities to connect your guests with each other. Be a connector, not just a networker.

7. **Follow Up Strategically**: After the event, don't let those connections fade. Send personalized follow-up emails to everyone who attended. Offer additional resources, invite them to stay connected, or suggest a follow-up meeting. This simple gesture can turn a one-time interaction into an ongoing professional relationship.

Remember, your book launch isn't just about celebrating your achievement—it's about leveraging that achievement to expand your network. By hosting a well-targeted event, you create opportunities for meaningful connections with the right people.

### Your Book as a Collaboration Catalyst
Your book isn't the end of a journey—it's the beginning of many new ones. It's a powerful catalyst for collaborations, but only if you use it strategically. Don't view your book as a finished product. Instead, see it as a conversation starter, a bridge to new partnerships and projects.

The key to initiating collaborations is to approach people with an offer, not a request. When you reach out to potential collaborators, lead with what you can offer them, not what you want from them. Your book gives you the credibility to make these offers.

For instance, if you're looking to connect with a thought leader in your industry, don't just send them your book with a vague hope of getting something in return. Instead, offer your book along with a specific suggestion for collaboration. Maybe it's a joint webinar, a co-authored article, or an interview series exploring the themes of your book.

Here's a template you could use:

"Dear [Thought Leader],

I've long admired your work in [specific area], and I believe there's an interesting overlap with the themes I explore in my recent book, [Title]. I'd love to send you a copy.
Moreover, I have an idea for a collaboration that I think could benefit both of us and our audiences. Would you be interested in [specific collaboration idea]? I believe it could provide valuable insights on [topic] for both our followers.
I'd be happy to discuss this further if you're interested. Thank you for your time and consideration."

Remember, networking isn't about taking—it's about creating mutually beneficial relationships. Your book is an entry point, but it's your follow-up and offer of collaboration that will turn a simple introduction into a long-term professional relationship.

## Maximizing Your Presence at Industry Events

Industry events are goldmines for expanding your professional network, and your book gives you a significant edge in these environments. Whether you're attending a conference, a trade show, or a networking mixer, your book should be an integral part of your strategy.

Here are five ways to leverage your book at industry events:

**1. Offer Your Book as a Giveaway**: If you're speaking at an event, offer copies of your book as part of your session. You can also host a booth or sponsor a giveaway to distribute your book to attendees. This ensures that your expertise is in their hands long after the event is over.

**2. Create a Discussion Around Your Book**: When meeting new people, bring your book into the conversation organically. Share a specific insight from your book that relates to the discussion at hand. This not only establishes your expertise but also piques their interest in reading more.

**3. Use Your Book as a Business Card**: Instead of (or in addition to) handing out business cards, give people copies of your book. It's more memorable and provides more value than a simple card.

**4. Host a Book-Themed Side Event**: During large industry conferences, host a small side event related to your book. This could be a breakfast discussion, a lunchtime workshop, or an evening reception. It gives people a reason to connect with you beyond the main event.

5. **Follow Up with a Signed Copy**: After the event, send a personalized, signed copy of your book to the key people you met. This reinforces the connection and gives them a reason to remember you.

Remember, the goal isn't just to hand out as many books as possible. It's to use your book as a tool for creating meaningful connections. Each book you give away should be accompanied by a genuine interaction and a plan for follow-up.

## Your Book, Your Network, Your Future

Your book is more than just a collection of your thoughts and ideas. It's a powerful networking tool that can open doors to new opportunities, collaborations, and professional relationships. Whether you're using it as an introduction at events, leveraging it for collaborations with influencers, or using it to create valuable experiences for your network, your book has the potential to dramatically expand your professional circle.

But remember, the book itself is just the beginning. It's what you do with it—how you use it to connect, collaborate, and create value for others—that will truly transform your network and your career.

As you continue on your publishing journey, keep these strategies in mind. Each interaction sparked by your book is a potential relationship that could lead to new opportunities. Your book isn't just a product—

it's a bridge to a whole new world of professional connections and possibilities.

## Your Next Chapter Starts Now

You've learned how your book can be a powerful tool for expanding your professional network. You've seen how it can open doors to new connections, collaborations, and opportunities. Now, it's time to put these strategies into action.

But you don't have to do it alone. At Ardith Publishing, we're committed to helping authors like you maximize the networking potential of your book. We offer guidance on everything from planning strategic book launches to leveraging your book at industry events.

Here's how you can take the next step:

1. **Sign up for the Ardith Publishing newsletter**: Get expert tips, networking strategies, and insider knowledge delivered straight to your inbox. Our newsletter is packed with valuable insights to help you use your book to build a powerful professional network.

2. **Contact Ardith Publishing**: Ready to take your networking efforts to the next level? Our team of experienced publishing professionals is here to help. We'll work with you to develop a customized strategy for using your book to expand your professional network and open doors to new opportunities.

Don't let another day pass without maximizing the

networking potential of your book. Your network is your net worth, and your book is the perfect tool to expand it.

Contact Ardith Publishing today. Let's work together to transform your book into a powerful networking tool that propels your career to new heights. Your next great professional connection could be just one book away.

Remember, in the world of business and networking, your book is your secret weapon. It's time to unleash its full potential. Are you ready to write the next chapter of your professional success story.

mike@ardithpublishing.com
www.ardithpublishing.com

# Chapter 4

## Enhancing Visibility and Brand Awareness - Your Book as a Beacon for Your Business

Imagine your book as a lighthouse. It stands tall, shining its beam across the vast ocean of your industry. This beacon doesn't just guide ships to shore—it attracts attention, sparks curiosity, and draws people to you. Your book isn't merely a collection of pages. It's a powerful tool that can illuminate your brand, making it impossible to ignore.

But here's the catch: lighthouses don't build themselves. They require careful planning, strategic positioning, and constant maintenance. Similarly, using your book to enhance visibility and brand awareness doesn't happen by accident. It requires intention, strategy, and consistent effort.

In this chapter, we'll explore how to transform your book from a simple product into a cornerstone of your brand. We'll dive into strategies that will make your book work overtime, attracting new audiences and cementing your position as a thought leader in your field. Get ready to turn up the wattage on your brand's visibility.

### Weaving Your Book into Your Brand's DNA

Your brand tells a story. It's not just about logos

and colour schemes—it's about the narrative you've crafted around your business, your values, and your unique approach. Your book should be a pivotal chapter in this ongoing story.

Think of your favourite brands. Apple isn't just about sleek gadgets; it's about innovation and thinking differently. Nike isn't selling shoes; it's inspiring athletic achievement. Your book should play a similar role for your brand. It's not a separate entity—it's an integral part of your brand's narrative.

Start by identifying the core themes of your brand. What do you want people to think of when they hear your name? If you're a leadership coach, perhaps your brand revolves around empowering others and fostering innovation. Your book should echo these themes, providing insights and strategies that reinforce your brand's core message.

Now, let's get practical. How do you align your book with your brand? Here's a step-by-step approach:

1. **Identify Your Brand's Core Values**: List out the fundamental principles that guide your business. These are the non-negotiables that define who you are and what you stand for.

2. **Articulate Your Brand's Mission**: What's the overarching goal of your business? What change are you trying to create in the world? Your book should contribute to this mission.

3. **Define Your Brand's Voice**: Is your brand serious and academic, or casual and approachable? Your

book's tone should match this voice.

**4. Link Your Book's Content to Your Brand's Offerings**: If you provide consulting services, your book should complement these services, not replace them. It should give readers a taste of your expertise while leaving them hungry for more.

**5. Craft a Unified Message**: Develop a concise statement that encapsulates both your brand and your book. This will be your go-to explanation when someone asks what you do.

Remember, every time someone picks up your book, they're interacting with your brand. Make sure it's a cohesive experience that reinforces who you are and what you stand for.

## Turning the Page on Media Opportunities

Media coverage is the megaphone that amplifies your brand's voice. It can catapult you from relative obscurity to industry prominence. And guess what? Your book is the perfect excuse to grab that megaphone.

But here's the truth: media opportunities rarely fall into your lap. You need to chase them down. Your book gives you the ammunition to do just that. You're not just another professional seeking attention—you're an author with valuable insights to share.

Let's break down the process of leveraging your book for media opportunities:

**1. Identify Your Media Targets**: Where does your

ideal audience hang out? Make a list of podcasts, blogs, magazines, and TV shows that cater to your target market. Be specific and realistic—starting with niche outlets can help you build momentum.

2. **Craft a Compelling Pitch**: Your pitch should answer one crucial question: "Why should our audience care?" Don't just say you've written a book. Explain how your insights can solve a problem or provide value to their audience.

3. **Tailor Your Approach**: Each media outlet is unique. A podcast might want entertaining stories, while a business journal may prefer hard data. Customize your pitch accordingly.

4. **Provide Ready-to-Use Content**: Make it easy for media outlets to feature you. Provide a press kit (more on this later), suggest interview questions, or offer to write a guest post based on your book's content.

5. **Follow Up Strategically**: Don't be discouraged by initial silence. Follow up after a week, providing additional information or a new angle on your story.

6. **Maximize Each Opportunity**: Once you land a media spot, make the most of it. Prepare thoroughly, be engaging, and always find a natural way to mention your book without being pushy.

Remember, media appearances aren't just about

promoting your book—they're about showcasing your expertise and building your brand. Focus on providing value, and the book promotion will happen organically.

## The Visual Symphony: Aligning Your Book's Look with Your Brand

In the world of branding, consistency is king. Your book's visual elements should harmonize perfectly with your existing brand identity. This visual consistency creates a seamless experience for your audience, reinforcing your professional image and building trust.

Think of your book as a visual ambassador for your brand. Every element, from the cover design to the font choices, should align with your brand's aesthetic. Here's how to ensure your book looks the part:

1. **Colour Scheme**: Use your brand's colour palette in your book cover and interior design. If your brand is known for vibrant blues and greens, incorporate these into your book's visuals.

2. **Typography**: If your brand uses specific fonts, carry these over to your book. Consistency in typography creates a subliminal connection between your book and your broader brand.

3. **Imagery Style**: Does your brand use photography, illustrations, or a mix of both? Your book should follow suit. If your website features clean, minimalist graphics, your book cover should echo this style.

**4. Logo Placement**: Subtly incorporate your logo into the book design. This could be on the spine, back cover, or as a watermark on chapter title pages.

**5. Overall Aesthetic**: If your brand is sleek and modern, your book should exude the same feel. If you're known for a more classic, timeless approach, let that influence your book's design.

Remember, you want people to recognize your book as part of your brand at a glance. Achieve this, and you've created a powerful visual tool for brand recognition.

### Your Press Kit: The Key to Media Doors

A well-crafted press kit is your ticket to media attention. It's a comprehensive package that gives journalists, bloggers, and podcast hosts everything they need to feature you and your book. Think of it as a one-stop shop for all things you and your brand.

Here's what your press kit should include:

**1. Author Bio**: Craft a compelling narrative about who you are and why you're qualified to write this book. Keep it concise but impactful.

**2. Book Synopsis**: Provide a brief, engaging summary of your book. Highlight the key problems it solves and the unique insights it offers.

**3. Sample Interview Questions**: Make it easy for

media hosts by suggesting thought-provoking questions they could ask you. This guides the conversation towards your areas of expertise.

4. **Key Talking Points**: List 3-5 main ideas from your book that you're comfortable discussing in depth. These should align with your brand's core message.

5. **High-Resolution Images**: Include professional headshots and high-quality images of your book cover. Provide options for both print and digital media.

6. **Past Media Appearances**: If you've been featured in the media before, include links or clips. This shows you're interview-ready and adds to your credibility.

7. **Contact Information**: Make it easy for media to reach you. Include your email, phone number, and relevant social media profiles.

8. **Testimonials or Endorsements**: If you have praise from industry leaders or early readers, include these to add weight to your credibility.

Your press kit should be easily accessible. Consider hosting it on your website and including a link in your email signature. The easier you make it for media to feature you, the more likely they are to do so.

## The Marie Forleo Effect: A Masterclass in Book-Driven Branding

Let's dive into a real-world example of book-driven brand building. Marie Forleo, with her book *Everything Is Figureoutable* didn't just write a best-seller—she orchestrated a brand explosion.

Forleo was already a successful online entrepreneur, but her book took her brand to new heights. Here's how she did it:

1. **Message Alignment**: Forleo's book title became her brand's rallying cry. *Everything is figureoutable* was more than a book title—it was a philosophy that permeated all aspects of her brand.

2. **Consistent Messaging**: Whether she was on a podcast, TV show, or social media, Forleo consistently returned to her core message. This repetition made her brand instantly recognizable.

3. **Multi-Platform Approach**: Forleo didn't rely on one medium. She leveraged podcasts, TV appearances, social media, and her own platforms to create a surround-sound effect for her message.

4. **Value-First Approach**: In every appearance, Forleo focused on providing value to the audience. This made her a sought-after guest and endeared her to new followers.

5. **Community Building**: Forleo used her book to strengthen her existing community and attract new members. She created book clubs, chal-

lenges, and interactive content that kept her audience engaged long after they finished reading.

The result? Forleo's book became more than a bestseller—it became a movement. Her brand awareness skyrocketed, and she positioned herself as a global thought leader in personal development and entrepreneurship.

## Your Book, Your Brand: Strategies for Synergy

Now that we've explored the components of using your book to enhance visibility and brand awareness, let's put it all together with some actionable strategies:

1. **Create a Book-Brand Tagline**: Develop a short, memorable phrase that encapsulates both your book's message and your brand's core value. Use this consistently across all platforms.

2. **Develop Signature Stories**: Identify 3-5 key stories or case studies from your book that best represent your brand. Polish these and use them consistently in interviews and speaking engagements.

3. **Launch a Multimedia Campaign**: Don't rely on just one medium. Create videos, podcast episodes, blog posts, and social media content that all tie back to your book's core message.

4. **Host Virtual Events**: Organize webinars, Q&A sessions, or online workshops based on your

book's content. These events can attract new audience members and reinforce your expertise.

5. **Collaborate with Influencers**: Identify influencers in your industry whose values align
with your book's message. Offer them advance
copies and encourage them to share their thoughts
with their audiences.

6. **Create Shareable Content**: Design quote
graphics, infographics, or short video clips based
on your book's key ideas. Make it easy for your
audience to share your message.

7. **Align Your Online Presence**: Update your website, social media profiles, and email signatures
to prominently feature your book and its core
message.

Remember, the goal is to create a seamless experience where your book and your brand are inextricably
linked in people's minds.

### Illuminating Your Brand's Future
Your book is more than words on a page—it's a
beacon for your brand. When strategically leveraged,
it can illuminate new paths for your business, attract
a wider audience, and cement your position as a
thought leader in your field.

But like any powerful tool, your book's effective-
ness in building your brand depends on how you use
it. Integrate it into your brand's story, align its visuals
with your brand identity, use it to create media oppor-

tunities, and consistently reinforce its message across all platforms.

Remember, publishing your book isn't the end of the journey—it's the beginning of a new chapter in your brand's story. Every media appearance, every social media post, every client interaction is an opportunity to reinforce the connection between your book and your brand.

**Your Next Chapter Awaits**

You've learned how your book can be a powerful catalyst for enhancing your visibility and brand awareness. You've seen how it can open doors to media opportunities, reinforce your brand identity, and elevate your professional status. Now, it's time to put these strategies into action.

But you don't have to navigate this journey alone. At Ardith Publishing, we specialize in helping authors like you leverage their books to build powerful, recognizable brands. We offer expert guidance on everything from crafting compelling press kits to aligning your book's message with your overall brand strategy.

Here's how you can take the next step:

1. **Sign up for the Ardith Publishing newsletter**: Get expert tips, branding strategies, and insider knowledge delivered straight to your inbox. Our newsletter is packed with valuable insights to help you use your book to enhance your visibility and build a powerful brand.

2. **Contact Ardith Publishing**: Ready to turn your book into a brand-building powerhouse? Our

team of experienced publishing professionals is here to help. We'll work with you to develop a customized strategy for using your book to enhance your visibility, build your brand, and open doors to new opportunities.

Don't let your book be just another title on a shelf. Let it be the beacon that guides your brand to new heights of recognition and success.

Remember, in the world of business and branding, your book is your secret weapon. It's time to unleash its full potential. Are you ready to let your brand shine?

mike@ardithpublishing.com
www.ardithpublishing.com

# Chapter 5

## Direct Sales and Revenue - Turning Your Book into a Money-Making Machine

Picture this: Your book, once just a glimmer in your mind's eye, now sits proudly on shelves (both virtual and physical) around the world. But here's the million-dollar question: Is it making you money? Writing a book is an achievement, but selling it—now that's an art form.

Welcome to the world of book sales, where strategy reigns supreme and creativity pays dividends. In this chapter, we'll unlock the secrets of turning your literary masterpiece into a cash-generating powerhouse. From pricing wizardry to distribution mastery, we'll explore the alchemy of transforming words into wealth.

Buckle up, dear author. We're about to embark on a journey that will transform you from a wordsmith into a sales savant. Let's dive in and discover how to make your book not just a bestseller, but a best-earner.

### The Art of Pricing: Finding Your Book's Sweet Spot

Pricing your book is like finding the perfect temperature for your morning coffee—too hot, and it burns; too cold, and it's unpalatable. Your goal? The Goldilocks zone of pricing: just right.

Set your price too high, and you'll watch potential readers scroll past your book faster than you can say "overpriced." Price it too low, and you risk readers questioning its value (not to mention shortchanging yourself). The key is to strike a balance that respects your expertise while enticing readers to click that "Buy Now" button.

So, how do you find this elusive sweet spot? Start by donning your detective hat and investigating your market. What are similar books in your genre priced at? This gives you a baseline, but remember—your book is unique. Maybe it offers groundbreaking insights or includes exclusive resources. These factors can justify a higher price point.

Consider your audience, too. Are they bargain hunters or luxury seekers? Price-sensitive students or professionals willing to invest in their growth? Understanding your readers' purchasing habits is crucial in setting the right price.

Now, let's talk strategy. One powerful approach is tiered pricing. Think of it as a three-course meal for your readers:

1. **Appetizer (Standard Edition)**: Your basic ebook or paperback. Priced competitively to attract a wide audience.

2. **Main Course (Special Edition)**: Includes bonus content like worksheets or video tutorials. Priced higher to reflect the added value.

3. **Dessert (Collector's Edition)**: Signed, limited edition with exclusive materials. Priced at a pre-

mium for your die-hard fans.

This tiered approach allows you to capture different segments of your market. Some readers will opt for the affordable standard edition, while others will happily splurge on the collector's edition. By offering options, you're maximizing your revenue potential.

Remember, pricing isn't set in stone. Don't be afraid to experiment. Try different price points and monitor your sales. The market will give you feedback—listen to it.

### Distribution Dilemma: Choosing Your Book's Path to Readers

In the world of book distribution, you're faced with a buffet of options. Each platform offers its own flavour of advantages and challenges. Your job? To create the perfect distribution recipe for your book's success.

Let's start with the elephant in the room: Amazon. It's the Goliath of book selling, offering unparalleled reach and visibility. With its Kindle Direct Publishing (KDP) platform, you can have your ebook available to millions of readers in a matter of hours. For print books, their print-on-demand service eliminates the need for costly inventory.

But Amazon's reach comes at a price. They'll take a hefty slice of your sales—anywhere from 30% to 70%, depending on your pricing and format. Plus, you'll have limited access to customer data, making it challenging to build direct relationships with your readers.

Next up: Barnes & Noble. While not as massive as

Amazon, B&N offers a solid alternative, especially for reaching U.S. readers. Their Nook platform provides another avenue for ebook sales, and their brick-and-mortar stores offer the potential for physical shelf space—a dream for many authors.

But what about cutting out the middleman altogether? Enter self-distribution. By selling directly through your website or at events, you keep a larger slice of the pie. You also gain complete control over pricing, promotions, and customer data. The downside? You're responsible for every aspect of fulfillment, from processing orders to shipping books.

So, what's an author to do? Here's a winning strategy: diversify. Start with Amazon for its unmatched reach. Then, expand to other platforms like Barnes & Noble to capture different market segments. Finally, set up a direct sales channel on your website for the highest profit margins and direct customer relationships.

Remember, each channel serves a purpose. Amazon might be your visibility booster, while your website becomes the hub for your most loyal readers. By leveraging multiple channels, you're casting a wider net and maximizing your book's earning potential.

### The Sales Funnel: Guiding Readers from Curiosity to Purchase

Imagine your book as a theme park ride. Your sales funnel is the line that guides eager visitors (your potential readers) from the entrance (awareness) to the exhilarating finale (purchase). The key? Making the journey so enticing that they can't resist going all the way to the end.

Let's break down this funnel into actionable steps:

**1. Awareness**: This is where you catch your reader's eye. Use social media, blog posts, or podcast appearances to put your book on their radar. Share intriguing snippets or behind-the-scenes insights to pique their curiosity.

**2. Interest**: Now that you have their attention, it's time to reel them in. Offer a free chapter or a related resource in exchange for their email address. This not only provides value but also gives you a direct line of communication with potential buyers.

**3. Consideration**: Keep nurturing that interest. Send a series of emails showcasing the unique value of your book. Share testimonials from satisfied readers or highlight specific problems your book solves.

**4. Intent**: At this stage, your potential reader is seriously considering a purchase. Sweeten the deal with a limited-time offer or exclusive bonus content for buyers.

**5. Purchase**: The moment of truth! Make the buying process as smooth as possible. Clear call-to-action buttons, multiple payment options, and a hassle-free checkout process are crucial.

**6. Post-Purchase**: The journey doesn't end with the sale. Follow up with a thank-you email, ask for reviews, and offer additional resources or upsells related to your book.

Here's where it gets exciting: upsells and cross-sells. Once a reader has shown interest in your book, you have the perfect opportunity to offer more value (and generate more revenue). Consider these ideas:

1. **Companion Workbook**: Offer a practical guide that helps readers implement the ideas from your book.

2. **Video Course**: Create a series of videos that dive deeper into your book's concepts.

3. **One-on-One Coaching**: For premium buyers, offer a personalized coaching session to help them apply your book's teachings.

By guiding readers through this carefully crafted funnel, you're not just selling a book—you're creating a comprehensive experience around your expertise.

## Pre-Orders, Bulk Sales, and Special Editions: The Trifecta of Book Revenue

Now, let's talk about three powerful strategies that can supercharge your book sales: pre-orders, bulk sales, and special editions. Think of these as the nitro boost for your book's revenue engine.

## Pre-Orders: Building Momentum Before Launch

Pre-orders are like the drumroll before the big reveal. They create anticipation, gauge interest, and can give your book a running start on launch day. Many platforms, including Amazon, count pre-orders towards your first-week sales, which can catapult your book up the bestseller lists.

To make your pre-order campaign irresistible, consider these tactics:

• Offer an early-bird discount for pre-order customers.

• Include exclusive bonuses like a private webinar or additional digital content.

• Create a "street team" of enthusiastic fans who help spread the word about your pre-order campaign.

## Bulk Sales: Tapping into the Corporate Gold Mine

Bulk sales are the hidden treasure of book revenue. Imagine selling 500 copies in one go instead of painstakingly marketing to individual readers. That's the power of bulk sales.

Target organizations that align with your book's message. If you've written a book on leadership, reach out to corporations for their management training programs. Written a book on wellness? Health clinics and yoga studios might be interested in bulk purchases for their clients.

Craft compelling bulk order packages:
• Offer tiered discounts based on order quantity.

• Include personalization options, like a custom foreword for the organization.

• Bundle in a speaking engagement or workshop with large orders.

## Special Editions: Creating Collector's Items

Special editions tap into the psychology of exclusivity. They're not just books; they're coveted items that true fans will clamor for.

Ideas for special editions:
• Hardcover versions with unique cover art.

• Signed and numbered limited editions.

• Deluxe packages that include additional materials like posters or exclusive digital content.

Price these editions at a premium. The perceived value and limited availability can justify a higher price point, significantly boosting your per-book revenue.

## Case Study: Brendon Burchard's The Motivation Manifesto

Let's look at a master of book sales in action. Brendon Burchard's launch of *The Motivation Manifesto* is a textbook example of effective sales strategies.

Burchard didn't just release a book; he orchestrated a multi-faceted campaign that maximized revenue at every turn:

**1. Pre-Order Campaign**: He offered irresistible bonuses for pre-orders, including access to an online course valued at several hundred dollars.

2. **Tiered Pricing**: Beyond the standard edition, Burchard offered a deluxe hardcover version at a premium price point.

3. **Bulk Sales**: He actively pursued corporate clients, offering customized packages for large orders.

4. **Upsells**: Buyers were offered additional products and courses related to the book's content, creating multiple revenue streams from a single customer.

5. **Continued Engagement**: Post-purchase, readers were invited to join a community, keeping them engaged and primed for future offers.

The result? *The Motivation Manifesto* became a New York Times bestseller, sold hundreds of thousands of copies, and generated millions in additional revenue through related offerings.

### Your Roadmap to Revenue: Actionable Steps for Maximizing Book Sales

Now that we've explored the strategies, let's create a roadmap for turning your book into a revenue-generating machine:

**1. Optimize Your Pricing**:
• Research your market thoroughly.
• Implement a tiered pricing strategy.
• Test different price points and analyze the results.

**2. Diversify Distribution**:
- Start with Amazon for maximum reach.
- Expand to other platforms like Barnes & Noble.
- Set up direct sales through your website.

**3. Craft Your Sales Funnel**:
- Create a compelling lead magnet (free chapter or resource).
- Develop an email nurture sequence.
- Design upsell and cross-sell offers.

**4. Launch with Impact**:
- Set up a pre-order campaign with exclusive bonuses.
- Recruit a "street team" to build buzz.
- Plan a series of launch events (virtual or physical).

**5. Pursue Bulk Sales**:
- Identify potential corporate or institutional buyers.
- Create attractive bulk purchase packages.
- Reach out personally to decision-makers.

**6. Create Scarcity and Exclusivity**:
- Design special edition versions of your book.
- Offer limited-time promotions.
- Create collector's items for super fans.

**7. Continual Optimization**:
- Regularly analyze your sales data.
- Gather feedback from readers.
- Iterate and improve your strategies based on results.

Remember, selling your book is an ongoing process. Stay flexible, be willing to experiment, and always keep your readers' needs at the forefront of your strategies.

## The Next Chapter in Your Book's Success Story

Congratulations! You've just unlocked the secrets to turning your book into a formidable revenue stream. You now have the tools to price strategically, distribute widely, and sell effectively. But remember, knowledge without action is like a book that never leaves the shelf—full of potential, but ultimately un-fulfilled.

Your book has the power to not only share your message but also to create a sustainable income that fuels your future endeavors. It's time to put these strategies into action and watch your book transform from a passion project into a profitable venture.

But you don't have to navigate this journey alone. At Ardith Publishing, we specialize in helping authors like you maximize the revenue potential of their books. Our team of experts can guide you through every step of the process, from pricing strategies to creating irresistible sales funnels.

Here's how you can take the next step in your book's success story:

1. **Sign up for the Ardith Publishing newsletter:** Get expert tips, proven sales strategies, and in-sider knowledge delivered straight to your inbox. Our newsletter is packed with valuable insights to help you turn your book into a steady stream of income.

2. **Contact Ardith Publishing**: Ready to supercharge

your book sales? Our team of experienced publishing professionals is here to help. We'll work with you to develop a customized sales strategy that aligns with your goals and maximizes your book's revenue potential.

Don't let your book's earning potential go unrealized. Your words have value—it's time to capture it.

Remember, in the world of book sales, knowledge is power, but action is king. Are you ready to reign over your book's financial future?

mike@ardithpublishing.com
www.ardithpublishing.com

# Chapter 6

## Using Your Book as a Lead Generation Tool - From Pages to Prospects

Imagine your book as a magnet. It attracts readers with its promise of knowledge, but its true power lies in its ability to draw those readers into your world. Your book isn't just a collection of ideas bound between two covers—it's a gateway, a bridge, a handshake extended to potential clients and customers. Welcome to the art of using your book as a lead generation tool.

In the bustling marketplace of ideas, your book stands out. It's a beacon of your expertise, a testament to your knowledge. But what if it could do more? What if, beyond sharing your insights, your book could become an active participant in growing your business? That's the magic of lead generation through your book.

Let's embark on a journey to transform your book from a static product into a dynamic tool that not only shares your wisdom but also builds lasting relationships with your readers. Get ready to unlock the hidden potential of your written words and watch as they become a powerful force in expanding your business horizons.

## Planting Seeds: Setting Up Lead Magnets Within Your Book

Your book is a garden of knowledge. Now, let's plant some seeds that will grow into flourishing client relationships. These seeds are lead magnets—irresistible offers sprinkled throughout your book that entice readers to connect with you beyond the page.

Lead magnets come in many forms. They can be as simple as a checklist or as complex as a video course. The key is to make them valuable, relevant, and impossible to resist. Here are some ideas to get your creative juices flowing:

1. **The Exclusive Chapter**: Offer an additional chapter that didn't make it into the final cut. This bonus content should be too good to miss.

2. **The Ultimate Toolkit**: Create a set of templates, worksheets, or resources that help readers implement your book's teachings.

3. **The Deep Dive Webinar**: Invite readers to a live or pre-recorded session where you expand on a key concept from your book.

4. **The Quick-Start Guide**: Develop a condensed version of your book's main ideas for readers who want to take action immediately.

5. **The Self-Assessment Quiz**: Design an interactive tool that helps readers evaluate their current status related to your book's topic.

But creating these lead magnets is only half the battle. The real art lies in how you present them within your book. You need to weave them into the narrative seamlessly, making them feel like a natural extension of the reading experience. Consider this approach:

**1. The Teaser**: Early in your book, hint at the valuable resources available to readers who want to go deeper.

**2. The Contextual Offer**: As you discuss a complex topic, mention your lead magnet as a tool to help readers navigate it.

**3. The Chapter-End CTA**: At the end of relevant chapters, remind readers about your lead magnet.

**4. The Grand Finale**: In your book's conclusion, make a compelling final offer for your most valuable lead magnet.

Remember, subtlety is key. Your lead magnets should enhance the reader's experience, not interrupt it. Use language that emphasizes the value readers will receive. For example:

"Want to implement these strategies right away? I've created a step-by-step action plan just for readers like you. Visit [yourwebsite.com/actionplan] to download it for free and start seeing results today!"

By strategically placing these offers throughout your book, you're creating multiple touchpoints for readers to connect with you. Each lead magnet is a bridge from the pages of your book to the broader world of your expertise.

## From Readers to Subscribers: Building an Email List

Congratulations! Your carefully crafted lead magnets have piqued your readers' interest. They've taken that crucial step from passive reader to active participant in your world. Now, it's time to nurture that budding relationship through the power of email marketing.

Your email list is more than just a collection of addresses. It's a direct line to people who have already shown interest in your ideas. These are your warmest leads, your most engaged audience. Treat them like the VIPs they are.

Start by making the sign-up process smoother than a freshly paved road. When readers follow the link from your book to your website, they should land on a page that's cleaner than a whistle and clearer than a bell. Here's what your landing page needs:

1. **A Headline That Pops**: Make it clear, compelling, and benefit-driven. "Unlock the Secrets to [Your Book's Main Benefit]" is more enticing than "Sign Up for My Newsletter."

2. **A Succinct Value Proposition**: In two or three sentences, tell readers exactly what they'll get and how it will improve their lives.

3. **A Form That's Short and Sweet**: Ask for the bare minimum—usually just a name and email address. Every additional field is another hurdle for potential subscribers.

**4. A Call-to-Action Button That Demands Attention**: Make it stand out visually and use action-oriented language. "Get My Free Guide Now" is more compelling than "Submit."

**5. A Sprinkle of Social Proof**: If you have testimonials or impressive numbers (like "Join 10,000+ subscribers"), include them to boost credibility.

Once a reader signs up, roll out the red carpet. Send them a welcome email faster than you can say "automated response." This email should:

**1.** Deliver the promised lead magnet

**2.** Thank them for joining your community

**3.** Set expectations for future communications

**4.** Invite them to connect with you on social media or other platforms

But don't stop there. Your welcome email is just the beginning of a beautiful friendship. Plan a series of follow-up emails that provide additional value and keep your new subscribers engaged. Share exclusive tips, behind-the-scenes insights, or sneak peeks at upcoming projects.

Remember, consistency is key in email marketing. Whether you choose to email your list weekly, biweekly, or monthly, stick to your schedule. Your subscribers should look forward to hearing from you, not wonder if you've fallen off the face of the earth.

## The Art of Nurture: Turning Subscribers into Clients

You've planted the seeds with your lead magnets. You've nurtured those seeds with your welcome sequence. Now it's time to watch your efforts blossom into client relationships. This is where the real magic of lead nurturing happens.

The key to successful nurturing is to always lead with value. Your subscribers didn't join your list to be bombarded with sales pitches. They're looking for solutions, insights, and inspiration. Give them what they want, and they'll give you their trust—and eventually, their business.

Here's a nurture sequence that can turn your book readers into loyal clients:

1. **The Value Bomb**: Start with an email that delivers unexpected value. Share an insight or strategy that's not in your book. Make your subscribers feel like they've stumbled upon hidden treasure.

2. **The Success Story**: Share a case study or testimonial that showcases how someone implemented your book's teachings successfully. This proves that your methods work in the real world.

3. **The FAQ Buster**: Address common questions or challenges your readers might face when applying your book's concepts. This positions you as a helpful guide on their journey.

4. **The Insider's Look**: Give your subscribers a peek behind the curtain. Share your personal experi-

ences, challenges, or "aha" moments related to your book's topic. This builds a deeper connection with your audience.

**5. The Soft Offer**: Introduce a low-risk offer that's a natural next step for readers who want to go deeper. This could be a webinar, a short consultation, or a mini-course.

**6. The Social Proof Parade**: Showcase more success stories and testimonials. Let your happy clients do the selling for you.

**7. The Direct Offer**: Finally, present your main offer. Whether it's one-on-one coaching, a comprehensive course, or a high-ticket service, frame it as the logical next step for those who are serious about achieving the results promised in your book.

Throughout this sequence, maintain the tone and style of your book. Your emails should feel like a continuation of the conversation you started in your book, not a jarring shift into sales mode.

### The Robbins Roadmap: Learning from a Master

Let's take a page from the playbook of a master: Tony Robbins. His book *Money: Master the Game* is a masterclass in lead generation. Robbins didn't just write a book—he created an entire ecosystem of value around it.

Throughout the book, Robbins strategically placed invitations to visit his website for additional resources. These weren't just afterthoughts—they were integral parts of the reading experience. Each offer felt like a natural extension of the chapter's content, providing readers with tools to implement Robbins' strategies immediately.

But Robbins didn't stop at lead generation. He created a nurture sequence that guided readers from free resources to paid programs seamlessly. He understood that the book was just the beginning of his relationship with readers

Here's what made Robbins' approach so effective:

1. **Relevance**: Each lead magnet was directly tied to the chapter's content, making it immediately useful to readers.

2. **Exclusivity**: The offered resources weren't available anywhere else, increasing their perceived value.

3. **Variety**: Robbins offered different types of lead magnets—calculators, worksheets, video content —catering to different learning styles.

4. **Segmentation**: By offering multiple lead magnets, Robbins could segment his email list based on readers' specific interests.

5. **Clear Value Proposition**: Each offer clearly stated how it would benefit the reader, making the decision to sign up a no-brainer.

6. **Seamless Integration**: The transition from book to website to email list felt natural and value-driven, not pushy or sales-y.

By following Robbins' example, you can create a lead generation system that feels less like marketing and more like a continuation of the value you provide in your book.

### Crafting Irresistible Lead Magnets: The Art of the Offer

Creating a lead magnet that readers can't resist is an art form. It's about understanding your audience's deepest desires and most pressing pain points. Your lead magnet should be the bridge between the knowledge in your book and the practical application of that knowledge in your reader's life.

Here's how to create lead magnets that have your readers scrambling to sign up:

1. **Solve a Specific Problem**: Don't try to boil the ocean. Focus on one specific challenge your readers face and solve it comprehensively.

2. **Make It Quick and Actionable**: In our fast-paced world, quick wins are golden. Create something readers can consume and apply in 15 minutes or less.

3. **Use a Compelling Title**: Your lead magnet's title should be so enticing that readers can't help but click. Use power words and be specific about the benefit.

4. **Over-Deliver on Value**: Make your free offer so good that readers wonder how amazing your paid offerings must be.

**5. Align with Your Book's Message**: Your lead magnet should feel like a natural extension of your book, not a disconnected afterthought.

**6. Make It Visually Appealing**: First impressions matter. Invest in professional design for your lead magnets.

**7. Offer Exclusive Insights**: Include information or strategies not found in your book to add extra value.

Remember, your lead magnet is often the first experience people have with your brand beyond your book. Make it count.

### The Landing Page: Your Digital Handshake

Your landing page is where the magic happens. It's where casual readers transform into engaged leads. Think of it as your digital handshake—it needs to be firm, confident, and leave a lasting impression.

Here are the key elements of a high-converting landing page:

**1. A Headline That Grabs Attention**: Your headline should speak directly to your reader's desires or pain points. Make it impossible to ignore.

**2. Compelling Copy**: Use clear, benefit-driven language that emphasizes what readers will gain. Keep it concise but persuasive.

**3. Strong Visuals**: Include an image or mockup of

your lead magnet. Let readers see what they're getting.

**4. Social Proof**: If you have testimonials or impressive stats, showcase them. Nothing sells like social proof.

**5. A Clear Call-to-Action**: Your CTA should stand out visually and use action-oriented language. Make it crystal clear what you want readers to do.

**6. Minimal Distractions**: Remove any elements that don't directly contribute to the sign-up goal. This includes navigation menus and external links.

**7. Mobile Optimization**: Ensure your landing page looks great and functions smoothly on all devices.

Test different versions of your landing page to see what resonates best with your audience. Small tweaks can lead to big improvements in conversion rates.

## Automation: Your 24/7 Lead Nurturing Assistant

In an ideal world, you'd personally welcome each new subscriber and guide them through your nurture sequence. But unless you've mastered cloning or time travel, that's not feasible. Enter automation—your tireless assistant in the lead nurturing process.

With the right tools, you can create a nurture sequence that feels personal and timely, even when it's running on autopilot. Here's how to set up an automated sequence that turns subscribers into clients:

**1. Choose the Right Tool**: Select an email marketing platform that offers robust automation features. Popular options include Mailchimp, ConvertKit, and ActiveCampaign.

**2. Map Out Your Sequence**: Plan your emails in advance, deciding on the content, timing, and goals for each message.

**3. Write Compelling Email Copy**: Craft emails that provide value, build trust, and gently guide subscribers towards your offers.

**4. Set Up Triggers and Conditions**: Use your email marketing tool to set up triggers (like signing up for your lead magnet) and conditions (like opening certain emails) to personalize the sequence.

**5. Include Strategic CTAs**: Each email should have a clear next step for subscribers, whether it's reading a blog post, watching a video, or exploring your services.

**6. Monitor and Optimize**: Regularly review your sequence's performance. Look at open rates, click-through rates, and conversion rates to identify areas for improvement.

Remember, automation is a tool, not a replacement for genuine connection. Infuse your automated emails with your personality and be ready to jump in personally when subscribers reach out.

## Your Book, Your Future: The Next Chapter

Congratulations! You've now unlocked the secrets of turning your book into a powerful lead generation tool. You've learned how to craft irresistible lead magnets, create high-converting landing pages, and nurture leads into loyal clients. But knowledge without action is like a book that never leaves the shelf—full of potential, but ultimately unfulfilled.

It's time to take what you've learned and apply it to your own book and business. Start by identifying the key insights in your book that could be transformed into valuable lead magnets. Then, craft a nurture sequence that guides your readers from casual interest to invested clients.

Remember, this process is a journey, not a destination. Continuously refine your approach, listen to your audience, and adapt your strategies as you grow.

But you don't have to navigate this journey alone. At Ardith Publishing, we specialize in helping authors like you maximize the lead generation potential of their books. Our team of experts can guide you through every step of the process, from creating compelling lead magnets to setting up automated nurture sequences.

Here's how you can take the next step in transforming your book into a lead generation powerhouse:

1. **Sign up for the Ardith Publishing newsletter**: Get expert tips, proven lead generation strategies, and insider knowledge delivered straight to your inbox. Our newsletter is packed with valuable insights to help you turn your book into a client attraction magnet.

**2. Contact Ardith Publishing**: Ready to supercharge your lead generation efforts? Our team of experienced publishing professionals is here to help. We'll work with you to develop a customized lead generation strategy that aligns with your book's message and your business goals.

Don't let your book's potential as a lead generation tool go untapped. Your words have the power to not only inform and inspire but also to build lasting relationships with readers who can become your most valued clients.

Contact Ardith Publishing today. Let's work together to transform your book from a one-time read into an ongoing source of high-quality leads for your business. Your book's most impactful chapter—the one where it becomes a client attraction magnet—is waiting to be written.

Remember, in the world of lead generation, your book is your most powerful ally. Are you ready to unlock its full potential?

mike@ardithpublishing.com
www.ardithpublishing.com

# Chapter 7

## Creating a Content Marketing Engine - Unleashing Your Book's Hidden Potential

Picture your book as a dormant volcano, brimming with untapped energy. Now, imagine that energy bursting forth, not in a destructive eruption, but in a dazzling display of content that illuminates the digital landscape. This is the power of turning your book into a content marketing engine. It's time to awaken the slumbering giant within your pages and let it roar across the internet.

Your book isn't just a static collection of words and ideas. It's a living, breathing entity capable of spawning countless pieces of content. Each chapter, every anecdote, and even the tiniest nugget of wisdom can be transformed into blog posts, videos, podcasts, and social media content that keep your audience engaged long after they've turned the last page. Welcome to the art of content repurposing—where one book becomes an endless stream of valuable insights.

In this chapter, we'll explore how to unleash your book's hidden potential and create a content marketing engine that runs on the fuel of your expertise. Get ready to turn your one-time publication into an evergreen source of engagement, authority, and business growth.

## From Chapters to Clicks: Transforming Your Book into Digital Gold

Let's start with the basics. Your book is a treasure trove of content, waiting to be mined. Each chapter is a goldmine of ideas that can be shaped into various forms of digital content. The key is to break down your book into digestible pieces that can be easily consumed in the fast-paced online world.

Start by dissecting your chapters. Look for key points, memorable quotes, and actionable tips. These will become the building blocks of your content marketing strategy. Here's how to turn those chapters into digital gold:

### Blog Posts: Your Book's Digital Echo

Blog posts are the workhorses of content marketing. They're SEO-friendly, shareable, and perfect for diving deeper into specific topics. Here's a simple process to turn your chapters into engaging blog posts:

1. **Identify Core Concepts**: Extract the main ideas from each chapter. These will form the backbone of your blog posts.

2. **Expand and Update**: Take those core concepts and flesh them out. Add new examples, recent statistics, or current events that relate to the topic. This keeps your content fresh and relevant.

3. **Break It Down**: Long chapters can often be split into multiple blog posts. This gives you more

content and allows you to explore topics in greater depth.

**4. Add a Personal Touch**: Include personal anecdotes or behind-the-scenes insights that weren't in the book. This gives readers a reason to engage with your blog even if they've read your book.

**5. Call to Action**: End each post with a clear next step for readers, whether it's to buy your book, sign up for your newsletter, or engage with you on social media.

Remember, blog posts don't have to be long to be effective. A 500-word post that delivers real value can be just as impactful as a 2000-word deep dive.

### Social Media: Bite-Sized Book Brilliance

Social media thrives on short, punchy content. It's the perfect place to share bite-sized nuggets of wisdom from your book. Here's how to turn your chapters into social media gold:

**1. Quote Mining**: Extract powerful quotes from your chapters. These can be turned into eye-catching graphics for platforms like Instagram or LinkedIn.

**2. Tip Sharing**: Condense actionable advice into short tips. These work great as Twitter threads or Facebook posts.

**3. Question Posing**: Use key concepts from your

book to spark discussions. For example, "In Chapter 3, I discuss the importance of failure in innovation. What's a failure that led to a big success for you?"

4. **Behind-the-Scenes**: Share insights about your writing process or stories that didn't make it into the book. This exclusive content keeps followers engaged and interested.

5. **Micro-Blogging**: Platforms like LinkedIn allow for longer posts. Use these to share condensed versions of your blog posts or book excerpts.

The key to social media success is consistency. Create a content calendar that ensures you're regularly sharing book-related content across your platforms.

### Lights, Camera, Action: Bringing Your Book to Life Through Video and Audio

In today's multimedia world, limiting your content to text is like painting in black and white when you have a full palette of colours at your disposal. Video and audio content allow you to bring your book's ideas to life in dynamic, engaging ways. They also cater to different learning styles and preferences among your audience.

### YouTube: Your Book's Visual Voice

YouTube is the second largest search engine in the world. By creating video content based on your book, you're tapping into a massive audience hungry for knowledge. Here's how to turn your chapters into compelling videos:

1. **Chapter Summaries**: Create short videos (5-10 minutes) summarizing the key points of each chapter. Think of these as video CliffsNotes for your book.

2. **Deep Dives**: Choose specific topics from your book and explore them in greater depth. This could be a series where you spend 15-20 minutes really digging into a concept.

3. **Q&A Sessions**: Host live Q&A sessions where viewers can ask questions about topics covered in your book. This interactive approach builds engagement and community.

4. **Behind the Scenes**: Share videos about your writing process, research methods, or personal stories related to the book's content. This gives viewers a more intimate connection with you and your work.

5. **Guest Interviews**: Invite experts mentioned in your book or colleagues in your field to discuss topics related to your book. This adds new perspectives and expands your reach.

Remember, you don't need Hollywood-level production values to create effective video content. A smartphone, decent lighting, and clear audio are often enough to get started.

## Podcasting: Your Book's Audio Adventure

Podcasts offer a unique way to expand on your book's content. They're perfect for busy professionals who want to learn while commuting, exercising, or doing chores. Here's how to turn your book into a compelling podcast series:

1. **Chapter Breakdowns**: Dedicate an episode to each chapter, diving deeper into the concepts and providing additional examples or case studies.

2. **Interview Series**: Invite experts, case study subjects, or readers to discuss topics from your book. This adds new voices and perspectives to your content.

3. **Listener Questions**: Dedicate episodes to answering listener questions about your book's content. This interactive approach keeps your audience engaged and provides valuable feedback.

4. **Behind the Microphone**: Share the story behind your book – why you wrote it, challenges you faced, and lessons you learned along the way.

5. **Book Club Style**: Host a virtual book club where you and guests discuss sections of your book in detail, almost like a director's commentary.

The beauty of podcasting is its intimacy. Your voice in your listeners' ears creates a personal connection that can deepen their engagement with your ideas.

## SEO Alchemy: Turning Book Content into Organic Traffic Gold

Now that you're creating a wealth of content from your book, it's time to ensure that content gets found. This is where Search Engine Optimization (SEO) comes into play. By optimizing your content for search engines, you can attract a steady stream of organic traffic to your website, blog, or YouTube channel.

Here's how to turn your book-based content into an SEO powerhouse:

1. **Keyword Research**: Use tools like Google Keyword Planner or Ubersuggest to identify keywords related to your book's topics. Focus on long-tail keywords that have decent search volume but lower competition.

2. **Optimize Content**: Incorporate these keywords naturally into your blog posts, video titles and descriptions, and podcast show notes. Remember, write for humans first, search engines second.

3. **Create Pillar Content**: Develop comprehensive guides or long-form articles that cover broad topics from your book. These can serve as 'pillar posts' that you link to from related, more specific content.

4. **Internal Linking**: Create a web of internal links between your content pieces. This helps search engines understand the structure of your site and the relationships between different topics.

**5. Meta Descriptions and Titles**: Craft compelling meta descriptions and titles for your content. These should include your target keywords and entice users to click through to your content.

**6. Optimize for Featured Snippets**: Structure your content to increase chances of appearing in featured snippets. Use clear headings, bullet points, and concise definitions of key terms.

**7. Create Transcripts:** For videos and podcasts, create text transcripts. This makes your content accessible to a wider audience and provides more text for search engines to index.

Remember, SEO is a long-term game. Consistency and quality are key. Keep producing valuable, optimized content, and you'll see your organic traffic grow over time.

### The Vaynerchuk Vortex: Lessons from a Content Repurposing Master

Let's take a moment to study a master of content repurposing: Gary Vaynerchuk. His book *Crush It!* became more than just a bestseller – it became the foundation for an entire content empire. Vaynerchuk didn't just write a book; he created a content vortex that continues to draw in new audiences years after publication.

Here's what we can learn from Vaynerchuk's approach:

**1. Micro-Content Creation**: Vaynerchuk is famous

for his "one becomes many" approach. He'll take a single piece of long-form content (like a chapter from his book) and turn it into dozens of social media posts, short videos, and graphics.

2. **Platform Diversity**: Vaynerchuk doesn't limit himself to one platform. He repurposes his content across YouTube, Instagram, LinkedIn, Twitter, and more – always adapting the content to fit each platform's unique characteristics.

3. **Consistency is Key**: Vaynerchuk maintains a relentless publishing schedule. By constantly putting out content, he stays top-of-mind for his audience and continually attracts new followers.

4. **Personal Branding**: Through his content, Vaynerchuk has built a strong personal brand that's inextricably linked to his books' messages. His personality shines through in every piece of content, creating a strong connection with his audience.

5. **Engagement Focus**: Vaynerchuk doesn't just broadcast content – he engages with his audience. He responds to comments, asks for feedback, and creates content based on his audience's questions and needs.

6. **Evergreen + Timely**: While much of his content is based on the evergreen principles from his books, Vaynerchuk also ties in current events and trends, keeping his content fresh and relevant.

By following Vaynerchuk's example, you can turn your book into a content marketing machine that continues to provide value and attract new readers long after its initial publication.

## Your Content Marketing Roadmap: From Book to Omnipresence

Now that we've explored the various ways to repurpose your book content, let's create a roadmap for turning your book into a long-term content marketing engine:

1. **Content Audi**t: Start by thoroughly reviewing your book. Create a spreadsheet listing each chapter, key concepts, memorable quotes, and actionable tips. This becomes your content reservoir.

2. **Platform Selection**: Decide which platforms align best with your target audience and personal strengths. Don't try to be everywhere at once – it's better to excel on a few platforms than to spread yourself too thin.

3. **Content Calendar Creation**: Develop a content calendar that outlines what you'll publish, where, and when. Aim for a mix of content types and topics to keep things interesting for your audience.

4. **Batch Creation**: Set aside time to create content in batches. This could mean writing several blog posts in one sitting or recording multiple video snippets in a single session. This approach is more

efficient and helps maintain consistency.

**5. Repurposing Workflow**: Establish a workflow for repurposing content. For example, a book chapter might become a long-form blog post, which is then broken down into several social media posts and a short video.

**6. Engagement Strategy**: Plan how you'll engage with your audience across different platforms. Will you host live Q&A sessions? Respond to every comment? Create a hashtag for discussions about your book?

**7. Measurement and Iteration**: Regularly review the performance of your content. Which pieces resonate most with your audience? Which platforms drive the most engagement? Use these insights to refine your strategy over time.

**8. Collaboration and Outsourcing**: Consider collaborating with other experts or outsourcing some content creation to scale your efforts. This could include hiring a video editor, a social media manager, or guest bloggers.

Remember, the goal is to create a sustainable content marketing engine that continues to drive interest in your book and your broader message. It's a marathon, not a sprint.

## Ignite Your Content Engine: Your Next Steps
Congratulations! You've just unlocked the secrets

to turning your book into a powerful content marketing engine. You now have the tools to transform your chapters into blog posts, social media content, videos, and podcasts. You understand how to optimize your content for search engines and have learned from the masters of content repurposing.

But remember, knowledge without action is like a book that never leaves the shelf – full of potential, but ultimately unfulfilled. It's time to put these strategies into action and watch your book's influence grow exponentially.

Your book is more than just a one-time publication – it's the fuel for an ongoing conversation with your audience. By consistently repurposing and sharing your book's content, you'll stay top-of-mind with your readers, attract new audiences, and establish yourself as a true thought leader in your field.

But you don't have to embark on this content marketing journey alone. At Ardith Publishing, we specialize in helping authors like you maximize the impact of their books through strategic content marketing. Our team of experts can guide you through every step of the process, from content planning to creation and distribution.

Here's how you can take the next step in your book's content marketing journey:

**1. Sign up for the Ardith Publishing newsletter:**
Get expert tips, proven content marketing strategies, and insider knowledge delivered straight to your inbox. Our newsletter is packed with valuable insights to help you turn your book into a content marketing powerhouse.

**2. Contact Ardith Publishing:** Ready to supercharge your content marketing efforts? Our team of experienced publishing professionals is here to help. We'll work with you to develop a customized content strategy that aligns with your book's message and your business goals.

Don't let your book's potential as a content marketing tool go untapped. Your words have the power to inform, inspire, and influence – it's time to amplify that power across multiple platforms and formats.

Remember, in the world of content marketing, your book is your most valuable asset. Are you ready to unleash its full potential?

mike@ardithpublishing.com
www.ardithpublishing.com

# Chapter 8

## Upselling with Premium Offers - Turning Readers into Raving Fans

Imagine your book as a key. It unlocks the door to a world of possibilities for your readers. But what lies beyond that door? That's where the real magic happens. Welcome to the art of upselling - the secret sauce that transforms casual readers into devoted clients and turns your book into a powerful business catalyst.

Your book is more than just ink on paper or pixels on a screen. It's the first step in a journey that can lead your readers to transformative experiences and you to greater success. By mastering the art of upselling, you're not just increasing your revenue - you're providing deeper value to those who are hungry for more of your expertise.

In this chapter, we'll explore how to turn your book into a gateway for premium offers. We'll dive into strategies for structuring your content, creating irresistible upsells, and guiding your readers towards high-value services that will change their lives - and your business.

## The Art of Subtle Persuasion: Structuring Your Book for Upsells

Your book is a story. It's a narrative of transformation, guiding readers from problem to solution. But what if the story doesn't end on the last page? What if it's just the beginning?

The key to effective upselling lies in how you structure your book. You need to create a narrative arc that naturally leads readers to want more. Here's how to do it:

1. **Start with a Bang**: Hook your readers from the first page. Present a compelling problem or vision that resonates deeply with them.

2. **Deliver Immediate Value**: Give your readers quick wins early in the book. This builds trust and keeps them engaged.

3. **Hint at Deeper Waters**: As you provide solutions, subtly indicate that there's more to explore. Use phrases like "We'll touch on this briefly here, but there's so much more to uncover."

4. **Showcase Success Stories**: Pepper your book with case studies of clients who've achieved amazing results through your premium services.

5. **Create Curiosity Gaps**: Introduce concepts that you don't fully resolve in the book. This creates a hunger for more information.

6. **End with a Call to Adventure**: Your conclusion

should feel like an invitation to the next stage of the journey.

Remember, the goal isn't to withhold information, but to create a natural progression. Your book should be valuable in its own right, while also whetting the reader's appetite for more.

Consider this structure:

**Chapter 1-3**: Establish the problem and your credibility.

**Chapter 4-6**: Provide valuable solutions and quick wins.

**Chapter 7-9**: Introduce more advanced concepts, hinting at their complexity.

**Chapter 10-12**: Showcase success stories and the transformative power of deeper work.

**Conclusion**: Invite readers to take the next step in their journey with you.

By structuring your book this way, you create a natural path from reader to client. It's not about hard selling - it's about inviting readers into a deeper relationship with you and your expertise.

## From Pages to Programs: Creating Irresistible Upsells

So, you've structured your book to prime readers for more. Now what? It's time to create upsells that feel like a natural extension of your book's value. Let's explore three powerful upsell options: webinars, courses, and coaching services.

## Webinars: Your Virtual Stage

Webinars are the perfect bridge between your book and higher-ticket offers. They allow readers to experience your expertise in real-time, creating a more personal connection. Here's how to create a webinar that converts:

1. **Choose a Focused Topic**: Pick one key concept from your book and dive deep. For example, if your book is about productivity, your webinar could be "The 3-Step System for Doubling Your Productivity in 30 Days."

2. **Provide Actionable Content**: Give attendees practical strategies they can implement immediately. This demonstrates the value of learning from you directly.

3. **Include Interactive Elements**: Use polls, Q&A sessions, and live demonstrations to keep attendees engaged.

4. **Create Scarcity**: Offer a special deal on your premium services that's only available to webinar attendees for a limited time.

6. **Follow Up**: Send recordings and additional resources to attendees, along with a time-sensitive offer for your premium services.

Remember, your webinar should feel like a natural extension of your book, not a hard sell. Provide massive value, and the sale will often make itself.

## Online Courses: Your Digital Classroom

If your book teaches a skill or system, an online course is a natural upsell. It allows readers to dive deeper into your methodology with structured, step-by-step guidance. Here's how to create a course that complements your book:

1. **Expand on Key Concepts**: Take the core ideas from your book and flesh them out with more examples, exercises, and advanced strategies.

2. **Use Multiple Media**: Include video lessons, downloadable worksheets, and interactive quizzes to cater to different learning styles.

3. **Offer Community**: Create a private forum or Facebook group where students can interact with each other and with you.

4. **Provide Accountability**: Include progress tracking and completion certificates to keep students motivated.

5. **Add Exclusive Content**: Include bonuses that aren't available in the book, like interviews with experts or deep dives into advanced topics.

Your course should feel like the "director's cut" of your book - all the great content, plus the behind-the-scenes insights and expanded scenes that superfans crave.

## Coaching: Your VIP Experience

For readers who want personalized guidance, coaching or consulting services are the ultimate up-sell. They offer the highest level of support and, often, the most transformative results. Here's how to position your coaching services:

1. **Highlight the Personalization**: Emphasize how coaching allows you to tailor your strategies to each client's unique situation.

2. **Showcase Results**: Share specific, quantifiable outcomes that past coaching clients have achieved.

3. **Offer Different Levels**: Create a tiered system, from group coaching to one-on-one VIP experiences, to cater to different budgets and needs.

4. **Provide a Taste**: Offer a free or low-cost strategy session to give potential clients a sample of what working with you is like.

5. **Create Exclusivity**: Position your highest-tier coaching as a selective program, requiring an application or invitation to join.

Your coaching offer should feel like the fast-track to success - the opportunity to work directly with the expert they've come to trust through your book.

## The Funnel of Fascination: Guiding Readers to Premium Offers

Now that you've got your upsells in place, how do you guide readers towards them? It's all about creating a seamless journey from book to premium offer. Let's break down the process:

1. **Plant Seeds in Your Book**: Throughout your book, subtly mention your premium offers. For example, "I guide my coaching clients through this process in much more detail."

2. **Create a Compelling CTA**: At the end of your book, include a clear call-to-action. Offer a free resource (like a workbook or video training) in exchange for the reader's email address.

3. **Nurture Through Email**: Once you have their email, send a series of value-packed messages that expand on the book's concepts and introduce your premium offers.

4. **Offer a Low-Cost Tripwire**: Create a low-priced offer (like a mini-course or toolkit) to convert readers into paying customers.

5. **Invite to a Webinar**: Host a free webinar that provides additional value and introduces your higher-ticket offers.

6. **Present Your Premium Offer**: At the end of the webinar, invite attendees to apply for your coaching program or join your comprehensive course.

7. **Follow Up**: For those who don't buy immediately, continue to provide value through email, social media, and retargeting ads.

The key is to make each step valuable in its own right. Your readers should feel like they're gaining something at every stage, whether or not they ultimately invest in your premium offers.

### The Brunson Blueprint: Lessons from a Master of Upsells

Let's take a page from the playbook of Russell Brunson, the founder of ClickFunnels and author of *Expert Secrets.* Brunson is a master of turning books into business-building machines. Here's what we can learn from his approach:

1. **Deliver Massive Value:** Brunson's books are packed with actionable strategies. Readers feel like they've gotten their money's worth before he ever mentions an upsell.

2. **Create a Movement**: Brunson doesn't just sell products; he invites readers to join a movement. His upsells feel like the next logical step for those who want to fully embrace his philosophy.

3. **Use Stories Effectively**: Throughout his books, Brunson shares stories of clients who've achieved success using his methods. These stories naturally lead readers to want similar results.

**4. Offer Multiple Entry Points**: Brunson provides various ways for readers to engage further, from free resources to high-ticket coaching programs.

**5. Create Urgency**: His offers often include time-sensitive bonuses, encouraging readers to take action quickly.

**6. Continuous Engagement**: Brunson uses email marketing, social media, and live events to keep his audience engaged long after they've finished his book.

By following Brunson's example, you can create a ecosystem of offers that naturally flow from your book, providing ongoing value to your readers and ongoing revenue for your business.

### The Psychology of Upgrade: Crafting Irresistible Offers

Understanding the psychology behind why people buy is crucial to creating effective upsells. Here are some key principles to keep in mind:

**1. Consistency**: People like to be consistent with their previous actions. If they've bought your book, they're more likely to buy related products from you.

**2. Loss Aversion**: People are more motivated by the fear of missing out than by potential gains. Frame your offers as limited-time opportunities.

**3. Social Proof**: We trust the actions of others. Use

testimonials and case studies to show that others have benefited from your premium offers.

4. **Reciprocity**: When you provide value (like in your book), people feel inclined to reciprocate. This makes them more open to your paid offers.

5. **Authority**: Your book establishes you as an authority. Leverage this perceived expertise when presenting your premium offers.

6. **Scarcity**: Limited availability increases perceived value. Consider offering exclusive bonuses or limited spots in your programs.

By understanding these psychological triggers, you can create offers that feel irresistible to your readers. Remember, it's not about manipulation - it's about aligning your offers with your readers' genuine desires and needs.

## From Reader to Raving Fan: Your Upsell Action Plan

You've got the strategies, you've seen the examples, now it's time to put it all into action. Here's your step-by-step plan for turning your book into a powerful upsell machine:

1. **Audit Your Book**: Review your manuscript (or outline, if you're still writing). Identify places where you can naturally hint at your premium offers.

2. **Create Your Ascension Model**: Map out your fun-

nel, from free resources to your highest-ticket offer. Ensure each step provides value and naturally leads to the next.

**3. Develop Your Upsells**: Based on your book's content, create webinars, courses, or coaching programs that expand on your core message.

**4. Craft Your CTAs**: Write compelling calls-to-action for your book, website, and marketing materials. Make it clear and easy for readers to take the next step.

**5. Build Your Follow-Up System**: Develop an email sequence that nurtures readers and introduces your premium offers.

**6. Test and Refine**: Launch your upsell system, then closely monitor results. Continuously refine your approach based on feedback and data.

Remember, the goal is to create a win-win situation. Your readers get more value, and you build a sustainable business around your expertise.

## Your Next Chapter Starts Now

Congratulations! You've just unlocked the secrets to turning your book into a powerful business-building tool. You now have the strategies to create compelling upsells, guide readers through your value ladder, and transform casual readers into devoted clients.

But remember, knowledge without action is like a

book that never leaves the shelf - full of potential, but ultimately unfulfilled. It's time to take what you've learned and apply it to your own book and business.

Your book is more than just a collection of ideas - it's the beginning of a journey that can transform both your readers' lives and your business. By creating thoughtful, valuable upsells, you're not just increasing your revenue - you're providing deeper support to those who are eager to learn more from you.

But you don't have to navigate this journey alone. At Ardith Publishing, we specialize in helping authors like you maximize the business-building potential of their books. Our team of experts can guide you through every step of the process, from structuring your book for natural upsells to creating and marketing your premium offers.

Here's how you can take the next step in transforming your book into a powerful upsell machine:

1. **Sign up for the Ardith Publishing newsletter:** Get expert tips, proven upsell strategies, and insider knowledge delivered straight to your inbox. Our newsletter is packed with valuable insights to help you turn your book into a client-attraction magnet.

2. **Contact Ardith Publishing:** Ready to supercharge your book's business-building potential? Our team of experienced publishing professionals is here to help. We'll work with you to develop a customized upsell strategy that aligns with your book's message and your business goals.

Don't let your book's potential as a business-building tool go untapped. Your words have the power to not only inform and inspire but also to create lasting, profitable relationships with your readers.

Remember, in the world of author entrepreneurship, your book is just the beginning. Are you ready to write your success story?

mike@ardithpublishing.com
www.ardithpublishing.com

# Chapter 9

## Creating Ancillary Products - Beyond the Book

Imagine your book as a seed. It contains within it the potential for a forest of opportunities. Now, picture that seed sprouting, growing, and blossoming into a vibrant ecosystem of products and experiences. This is the power of ancillary products - the offshoots that extend your book's reach and impact far beyond its pages.

Your book is not the end of the journey. It's the beginning of an adventure that can lead to a multitude of complementary products, each designed to deepen your readers' engagement and enhance their experience. From online courses to branded merchandise, these ancillary offerings do more than just increase your revenue - they provide additional avenues for your audience to interact with your ideas, implement your strategies, and immerse themselves in your world.

In this chapter, we'll explore how to transform your book into a launchpad for a diverse range of products that will amplify your message, expand your brand, and create multiple streams of income. Get ready to unlock the hidden potential of your book and turn it into a thriving ecosystem of value.

## From Pages to Pixels: Transforming Your Book into Digital Learning Experiences

In today's digital age, learning extends far beyond the printed page. Your readers are hungry for interactive, immersive experiences that bring your book's concepts to life. Let's explore how to satisfy that hunger by creating online courses and workshops that transform passive readers into active learners.

### Crafting an Online Course: Your Book's Digital Doppelganger

An online course is like your book's more outgoing twin. It takes the knowledge within your pages and presents it in a dynamic, engaging format that appeals to different learning styles. Here's how to bring your book to life in the digital realm:

1. **Map Your Book's DNA**: Start by breaking down your book into its core components. Each chapter can become a module, each key concept a lesson. This creates a natural structure for your course.

2. **Add Multimedia Magic**: Bring your content to life with videos, audio clips, and interactive elements. Record yourself explaining complex concepts, create animations to illustrate processes, or develop quizzes to reinforce learning.

3. **Create Action Steps**: Transform passive reading into active doing. Develop worksheets, assignments, and projects that allow students to apply what they've learned. This turns knowledge into

action.

**4. Foster Community**: Create a space for students to interact, such as a private Facebook group or forum. This builds a sense of community and allows for peer-to-peer learning.

**5. Offer Personal Touches**: Include live Q&A sessions or office hours where students can interact with you directly. This adds value and creates a more personal connection.

Remember, your course isn't just a rehash of your book. It's an expansion, an exploration, a deeper dive into the world you've created. Use the digital format to its fullest potential, offering experiences that simply aren't possible within the confines of a printed page.

### Workshops: Where Your Book Comes to Life

If an online course is your book's digital twin, a workshop is its three-dimensional manifestation. It's a space where your ideas leap off the page and into the real world, where readers become doers, and where you can witness the impact of your work first-hand.

Here's how to create a workshop that turns your book into a live, interactive experience:

**1. Choose Your Focus**: Pick a specific aspect of your book to explore in depth. This could be a particularly challenging concept, a practical skill, or a transformative process.

**2. Design Interactive Elements**: Create exercises, group discussions, and hands-on activities that allow participants to engage with your material in a tangible way.

**3. Prepare Visual Aids**: Develop slides, handouts, or physical props that support your teaching and make complex ideas more accessible.

**4. Plan for Different Learning Styles**: Include a mix of visual, auditory, and kinesthetic elements to cater to diverse learning preferences.

**5. Create Takeaways**: Provide participants with tangible tools they can use after the workshop, such as workbooks, checklists, or action plans.

**6. Follow-Up Strategy**: Design a follow-up system to support participants in implementing what they've learned, such as email check-ins or a private online community.

Whether held in person or virtually, workshops offer a unique opportunity to deepen your connection with your audience and see your ideas in action. They transform the solitary act of reading into a shared, communal experience of learning and growth.

### Tangible Touchpoints: Developing Physical Products That Embody Your Message

While digital products offer incredible reach and scalability, there's something special about physical items that readers can touch, use, and integrate into their daily lives. These tangible products serve as constant reminders of your book's message, keeping your ideas front and center in your readers' worlds.

## Tools of Transformation: Planners, Workbooks, and Practical Aids

If your book teaches a process, advocates for a lifestyle change, or promotes personal growth, consider creating physical tools that help readers implement your ideas. These could include:

1. **Custom Planners**: Design a planner that incorporates your book's principles into daily, weekly, or monthly planning. For instance, if your book is about productivity, create a planner that includes space for goal-setting, priority management, and reflection - all based on your unique system.

2. **Interactive Workbooks**: Develop a companion workbook filled with exercises, prompts, and space for reflection. This turns your book from a passive read into an active, personalized journey.

3. **Specialized Tools**: Create unique tools that support your book's methodology. If your book is about mindfulness, you might create a beautiful timer for meditation sessions. If it's about nutrition, consider designing a portion control plate or a meal planning kit.

4. **Card Decks**: Transform key concepts or exercises from your book into a deck of cards. These could

be inspirational quotes, daily challenges, or prompts for journaling or group discussions.

Remember, the key is to create items that are not just branded merchandise, but functional tools that genuinely help your readers apply your book's teachings in their everyday lives.

## Wearable Wisdom: Branded Merchandise That Spreads Your Message

Sometimes, the most powerful way to spread your message is to let your readers become walking billboards for your ideas. Branded merchandise not only generates additional revenue but also creates a sense of community among your readers. Here are some ideas:

1. **Inspiring Apparel**: Create t-shirts, hoodies, or hats featuring powerful quotes or key concepts from your book. Choose designs that not only look good but also spark conversations.

2. **Everyday Items**: Develop useful items like mugs, water bottles, or tote bags that incorporate your book's branding or message. These serve as daily reminders of your ideas.

3. **Office Supplies**: If your book is business-focused, consider creating branded notebooks, pens, or desk accessories that professionals can use in their work environments.

4. **Artistic Pieces**: For books with a strong visual or

inspirational component, create posters, wall art, or even jewelry that embodies your message in an aesthetic way.

The key to successful branded merchandise is to create items that your readers would want to use or wear even if they weren't connected to your book. Focus on quality, design, and alignment with your book's message and values.

### The Art of the Pitch: Marketing Your Ancillary Products

Creating amazing ancillary products is only half the battle. The other half is getting them into the hands of your readers. Let's explore strategies for effectively marketing your book's offspring.

### Your Book as a Launchpad

Your book itself is the perfect platform for introducing readers to your ancillary products. Here's how to leverage it:

1. **Strategic Mentions**: Weave references to your products naturally throughout the book. For example, "To help you implement this strategy, I've created a companion workbook available at [your website]."

2. **End-of-Chapter CTAs**: At the end of relevant chapters, include a call-to-action directing readers to related products or resources.

3. **Resource Section**: Include a comprehensive resource section at the end of your book that lists

all available ancillary products and how to access them.

**4. QR Codes**: For physical books, consider including QR codes that readers can scan to directly access your product pages or exclusive offers.

## Digital Domination: Leveraging Online Platforms
The digital world offers countless opportunities to showcase your ancillary products. Here's how to make the most of them:

**1. Dedicated Landing Pages**: Create specific landing pages for each product, optimized for SEO and conversions.

**2. Email Marketing**: Use your email list to introduce new products, offer exclusive deals, and share success stories from users.

**3. Social Media Campaigns**: Develop a social media strategy that highlights your products, including behind-the-scenes looks, user testimonials, and limited-time offers.

**4. Influencer Partnerships**: Collaborate with influencers in your niche to review or promote your products to their audiences.

**5. Content Marketing**: Create blog posts, videos, or podcast episodes that provide value while naturally introducing your products as solutions to common challenges.

## Bundling for Success

Bundling your book with ancillary products can be a powerful strategy to increase sales and provide added value. Consider these bundling ideas:

1. **Starter Pack**: Offer your book bundled with a companion workbook or planner at a slight discount.

2. **Digital + Physical**: Bundle your physical book with access to your online course for a comprehensive learning experience.

3. **Seasonal Specials:** Create themed bundles for holidays or special occasions, combining your book with relevant merchandise or tools.

4. **Corporate Packages**: Develop bulk packages for businesses, including your book, workbooks, and access to a private workshop for their team.

Remember, the key to successful bundling is to create packages that offer clear value and solve specific problems for your readers.

## Case Study: Chris Guillebeau's '$100 Startup' Empire

Let's draw inspiration from Chris Guillebeau, author of *The $100 Startup*, who masterfully turned his book into a thriving ecosystem of products and experiences.

Guillebeau didn't stop at writing a bestseller. He created a universe around his book's core concept of low-cost entrepreneurship. Here's how he did it:

**1. Online Community**: He launched the "100 Startup" forum, a paid membership site where aspiring entrepreneurs could connect, share ideas, and get personalized advice.

**2. Live Events**: Guillebeau organized the "World Domination Summit," an annual gathering that brought his book's principles to life through workshops, speakers, and networking opportunities.

**3. Online Courses**: He developed several courses, including "Adventure Capital," which expanded on the book's concepts and provided step-by-step guidance for starting a business.

**4. Toolkit**: Guillebeau created a digital "Empire Building Kit," a comprehensive resource for turning side hustles into full-time businesses.

**5. Podcast**: He launched the "Side Hustle School" podcast, which kept his audience engaged with daily episodes about starting small businesses.

By creating this diverse range of ancillary products, Guillebeau was able to cater to different learning styles, price points, and levels of engagement. He transformed *The $100 Startup* from a single book into a movement, providing ongoing value to his readers and multiple streams of income for himself.

## Identifying Your Ancillary Product Sweet Spot

Not all ancillary products are created equal. The key is to develop offerings that align perfectly with your book's message, your audience's needs, and your own strengths. Here's how to find your sweet spot:

1. **Analyze Your Book**: Identify the core problems your book solves and the key actions it encourages readers to take. These are prime areas for ancillary product development.

2. **Survey Your Audience**: Ask your readers directly what kinds of tools or resources would help them implement your book's ideas. Their answers might surprise you and lead to innovative product ideas.

3. **Assess Your Strengths**: Consider your own skills and interests. If you love public speaking, workshops might be a great fit. If you're tech-savvy, an online course could play to your strengths.

4. **Research Your Market**: Look at what other authors in your niche are offering. How can you differentiate yourself or fill gaps in the market?

5. **Start Small and Iterate**: Begin with one or two ancillary products and gather feedback. Use this information to refine your offerings and develop new ones.

Remember, the goal is to create products that not

only generate revenue but also genuinely enhance your readers' experience and help them achieve the outcomes promised in your book.

## Your Ancillary Product Action Plan

You've explored the world of ancillary products, from online courses to branded merchandise. Now it's time to take action. Here's your step-by-step plan to expand your book's impact:

1. **Brainstorm Ideas**: List all possible ancillary product ideas related to your book. Don't censor yourself - let your creativity flow.

2. **Prioritize Opportunities**: Evaluate each idea based on potential impact, alignment with your book, and feasibility. Choose the top 1-3 to focus on initially.

3. **Develop a Prototype**: Create a basic version of your chosen product(s). This could be an outline for a course, a design for merchandise, or a draft of a workbook.

4. **Gather Feedback**: Share your prototype with a small group of trusted readers or colleagues. Use their input to refine your product.

5. **Create a Marketing Plan**: Develop a strategy for introducing your ancillary product to your audience, including how you'll leverage your book to promote it.

**6. Launch and Learn**: Release your product and pay close attention to the response. Be prepared to make adjustments based on real-world feedback.

**7. Expand Thoughtfully**: As you see success, gradually introduce new ancillary products, always ensuring they align with your book's core message and your readers' needs.

Remember, creating ancillary products is an ongoing process of innovation and refinement. Stay connected to your audience's needs and be willing to evolve your offerings over time.

### Your Next Chapter Awaits

Congratulations! You've just unlocked the secrets to expanding your book's impact through ancillary products. You now have the tools to create online courses, develop physical products, and market your offerings effectively. You've seen how authors like Chris Guillebeau have built entire ecosystems around their books, and you have a roadmap to do the same.

But remember, knowledge without action is like a book that never leaves the shelf - full of potential, but ultimately unfulfilled. It's time to take what you've learned and apply it to your own book and business.

Your book is more than just a collection of pages - it's the seed of a potentially vast and vibrant product ecosystem. By creating thoughtful, valuable ancillary products, you're not just increasing your revenue streams - you're providing deeper support to those who resonate with your message and want to fully implement your ideas in their lives.

But you don't have to navigate this journey alone. At Ardith Publishing, we specialize in helping authors like you maximize the potential of their books through strategic ancillary product development. Our team of experts can guide you through every step of the process, from ideation to creation to marketing.

Here's how you can take the next step in transforming your book into a thriving product ecosystem:

1. **Sign up for the Ardith Publishing newsletter:** Get expert tips, proven strategies for ancillary product development, and insider knowledge delivered straight to your inbox. Our newsletter is packed with valuable insights to help you expand your book's impact and reach.

2. **Contact Ardith Publishing:** Ready to turn your book into the foundation of a diverse product line? Our team of experienced publishing professionals is here to help. We'll work with you to develop a customized strategy for creating and marketing ancillary products that align with your book's message and your business goals.

Don't let your book's potential as a launchpad for multiple products go untapped. Your words have the power to change lives in many forms - from digital courses to physical tools to inspiring merchandise.

Remember, in the world of publishing and entrepreneurship, your book is just the beginning. Are you ready to write the next chapter of your success story?

# Chapter 10

## International Markets and Rights Sales - Taking Your Book Global

Picture this: Your book, once confined to the shelves of local bookstores, now sits proudly in a Tokyo bookshop, its cover adorned with elegant Japanese characters. A German executive quotes a passage during a board meeting in Berlin. A classroom in Brazil buzzes with discussion about your ideas. This isn't a dream—it's the potential reality of tapping into international markets and rights sales.

Going global with your book isn't just about seeing your name in different languages (though that's undeniably cool). It's about expanding your reach, multiplying your income streams, and spreading your message to corners of the world you've never imagined. In this chapter, we'll embark on a journey to transform your book from a local sensation into a global phenomenon.

### The World is Your Oyster: Identifying Global Opportunities

Before you can conquer the world, you need to know where to plant your flag. Not every market will be ripe for your book's message, but with the right approach, you can uncover hidden gems of opportunity across the globe.

Start by asking yourself: What universal truths does my book contain? Books that tackle timeless human experiences—love, ambition, fear, hope—often transcend cultural boundaries with ease. A guide to effective leadership might resonate in boardrooms from New York to New Delhi. A novel exploring family dynamics could touch hearts in London and Lagos alike.

But don't stop at universal themes. Look for specific connections between your book and potential markets. Did you write a historical novel set in 19th century Japan? The Japanese market might be especially receptive. Is your self-help book based on ancient Greek philosophy? Greece could be an excellent starting point for your international journey.

Research is your compass in this global expedition. Dive into international publishing trends. Which countries have a voracious appetite for your genre? Where are literacy rates on the rise, creating new markets of eager readers? Tools like the Frankfurt Book Fair's annual reports or Publishers Weekly's international section can be goldmines of information.

Consider emerging markets too. Countries like India, with its rapidly growing middle class and increasing English proficiency, could be fertile ground for your book. China's massive population and expanding book market might be your ticket to exponential growth.

But remember, numbers aren't everything. Sometimes, a smaller market with a passionate interest in your book's subject matter can be more valuable than a larger, more general audience. A book about sustainable agriculture might find a dedicated following in eco-conscious Scandinavia, even if the population is smaller than other potential markets.

## The Art of the Deal: Selling Foreign Rights

Now that you've identified promising markets, it's time to make your move. Selling foreign rights is like playing chess on a global board—it requires strategy, foresight, and sometimes a bit of luck.

First, let's demystify the process. When you sell foreign rights, you're essentially granting a publisher in another country the right to translate, publish, and distribute your book in their territory. In return, you receive an advance (a lump sum upfront) and royalties on sales. It's a win-win: you expand your reach without having to navigate the complexities of foreign publishing yourself.

But how do you get started? Unless you're fluent in multiple languages and have a rolodex full of international publishing contacts, your best bet is to enlist the help of a foreign rights agent. These specialized agents are the secret weapon in your global expansion arsenal. They speak the language (sometimes literally) of international publishing deals and have networks spanning the globe.

Finding the right foreign rights agent is crucial. Look for someone with experience in your genre and connections in the markets you're targeting. A good agent will not only negotiate deals but also help you position your book for different cultural contexts. They might suggest tweaks to your title or cover to make it more appealing in specific markets.

Once you have an agent, they'll create a rights

guide—a sleek, professional document that showcases your book's potential to foreign publishers. This guide is your book's passport, containing a compelling synopsis, author bio, sales figures, and any accolades or reviews. It's designed to make foreign publishers sit up and take notice.

Now comes the exciting part: book fairs. The Frankfurt Book Fair and the London Book Fair are the Super Bowls of international publishing. Here, rights agents and publishers from around the world gather to buy and sell rights. Your agent will set up meetings, pitch your book, and hopefully spark bidding wars among interested publishers.

But what if you can't attend these fairs? Don't worry. Many deals happen year-round through online submissions and virtual meetings. Your agent will be your advocate, tirelessly promoting your book to their international contacts.

When offers start rolling in, it's time to negotiate. Advances for foreign rights can range from a few hundred dollars to six figures for highly sought-after books. Royalty rates typically fall between 5% to 10% of the book's price in the foreign market. Your agent will help you navigate these negotiations, ensuring you get the best possible deal.

Remember, selling foreign rights is often a long game. It might take months or even years to see results. But when you do, the payoff can be substantial—both financially and in terms of your global reach.

## Beyond Books: Licensing Content for Corporate and Educational Use

Your book's potential extends far beyond traditional publishing. Imagine your ideas shaping corporate strategies or molding young minds in classrooms around the world. This is the power of licensing your content for corporate and educational use.

Corporate licensing is like giving your book a corner office. Many companies are hungry for high-quality content to fuel their training programs. If you've written a book on leadership, time management, or innovative thinking, you could be sitting on a gold mine. Large corporations might license your content to train thousands of employees, providing you with a substantial new revenue stream.

To tap into this market, start by identifying companies or industries that align with your book's themes. Create a tailored licensing proposal that shows how your content can address specific corporate challenges. For example, if your book is about effective communication, highlight how it can improve team dynamics and customer relations.

Educational licensing opens doors to classrooms and lecture halls worldwide. Universities, schools, and online learning platforms are always on the lookout for fresh, engaging content. Your book could become required reading for business students in Singapore or part of an online course reaching learners in dozens of countries.

To make your book more attractive for educational licensing, consider developing supplementary materials. Create lecture slides, discussion questions, or even video content to accompany your book. This added value can make your offering irresistible to educators.

Licensing deals can take various forms. You might receive a flat fee for unlimited use of your content, or you could negotiate a per-user fee based on the number of employees or students accessing your material. Some deals might combine upfront payments with ongoing royalties.

Remember, the key to successful licensing is flexibility. Be open to adapting your content for different uses. A chapter from your book might become a standalone training module, or your key concepts could be transformed into an interactive online course.

## The Rowling Effect: Lessons from a Global Phenomenon

No discussion of international book success would be complete without mentioning J.K. Rowling and the Harry Potter series. While Rowling's level of success is rare, her journey offers valuable lessons for any author looking to expand globally.

Rowling's success wasn't just about writing a great story (though that certainly helped). It was about creating a brand that could be adapted and marketed across diverse cultures. The Harry Potter books were translated into over 80 languages, from Albanian to Zulu. But it didn't stop there. The brand expanded into movies, merchandise, and even theme park attractions.

The key takeaway? Think beyond the book. Your story or ideas could be the foundation for a much larger brand. As you enter new markets, consider how your book's concepts could be adapted into different media or products. Could your self-help book become a popular app in tech-savvy South Korea? Might your fantasy novel inspire a line of artisanal teas in England?

Rowling's success also highlights the importance of universal themes. While the Harry Potter books were steeped in British culture, they touched on universal experiences of friendship, courage, and coming-of-age that resonated worldwide. As you write and market your book, consider how its themes can connect with readers across different cultures.

## Your Global Expansion Roadmap

Ready to take your book global? Here's your step-by-step guide to international expansion:

1. **Assess Your Book's Global Potential**: Identify universal themes and specific cultural connections that could appeal to international markets.

2. **Research Target Markets**: Use publishing industry reports and cultural insights to pinpoint promising countries for your book.

3. **Find a Foreign Rights Agent**: Look for an agent with experience in your genre and connections in your target markets.

4. **Create a Compelling Rights Guide**: Work with your agent to develop a professional document that showcases your book's international potential.

**5. Attend (or Send Your Agent to) International Book Fairs**: These events are crucial for making connections and selling rights.

**6. Consider Licensing Opportunities**: Explore options for corporate and educational licensing to maximize your book's potential.

**7. Adapt and Localize**: Be open to tweaking your book's title, cover, or content to suit different cultural contexts.

**8. Build Your International Platform**: Use social media and your website to connect with readers in your target markets.

**9. Stay Informed**: Keep up with international publishing trends and emerging markets to identify new opportunities.

**10. Be Patient and Persistent**: Global expansion takes time. Stay committed to your international strategy for the long haul.

Remember, going global is a journey, not a destination. Each new market you enter is an opportunity to learn, grow, and expand your reach as an author.

## Your Passport to Global Success Awaits

Congratulations! You've just unlocked the secrets to taking your book global. You now have the tools to identify international opportunities, sell foreign rights, and explore lucrative licensing deals. You've seen how authors like J.K. Rowling have built global empires from their books, and you have a roadmap to start your own international journey.

But remember, knowledge without action is like a passport that never gets stamped. It's time to take what you've learned and apply it to your own book and career. Your words have the power to cross borders, bridge cultures, and touch lives around the world. The global stage is set—it's time for you to step into the spotlight.

However, navigating the complex world of international publishing doesn't have to be a solo adventure. At Ardith Publishing, we specialize in helping authors like you maximize the global potential of their books. Our team of experts can guide you through every step of the process, from identifying promising markets to negotiating foreign rights deals.

Here's how you can take the next step in your book's international journey:

1. **Sign up for the Ardith Publishing newsletter:** Get expert tips, insights on global publishing trends, and strategies for international success delivered straight to your inbox. Our newsletter is your passport to the latest information on taking your book global.

2. **Contact Ardith Publishing:** Ready to see your book in bookstores from Berlin to Beijing? Our team of experienced publishing professionals is here to help. We'll work with you to develop a customized strategy for international expansion

that aligns with your book's unique potential and your career goals.

Don't let borders limit your book's impact. Your words have the power to resonate with readers around the world—it's time to let them soar.

Remember, in the world of publishing, thinking globally isn't just an option—it's an opportunity. Are you ready to take your book on a world tour?

mike@ardithpublishing.com
www.ardithpublishing.com

# Chapter 11

## Conclusion - From Ink to Empire

You've done it. You've poured your heart, soul, and expertise onto the page. But here's the secret: your journey isn't ending—it's just beginning. Your book isn't merely a collection of words; it's a launchpad, a credential, a business card that never stops working. It's the foundation of what could become your empire.

Throughout this guide, we've explored the myriad ways your book can transform your business. From boosting your credibility to generating new revenue streams, from opening doors you never knew existed to taking your brand global, your book is the key that unlocks a world of possibilities. But possibilities mean nothing without action. So let's reflect on this journey and chart the course for your next chapter—the one where you become not just an author, but a mogul in your field.

### The Alchemy of Authorship: Turning Words into Gold

Writing a book is impressive. But you know what's more impressive? Leveraging that book to establish yourself as the go-to expert in your field. Your book is the modern-day equivalent of turning lead into gold—it transforms your knowledge into a tangible asset that elevates you above the crowd.

Think about it. When you hand someone your book, you're not just giving them paper and ink. You're offering them a piece of your mind, literally. It's as if you're saying, "Here, I've distilled years of experience and insight into these pages. This is what I know, and this is how I can help you." That's powerful. It's a level of credibility that a business card or a well-designed website simply can't match.

But here's the catch: credibility isn't automatic. Your book needs to deliver real value. It should solve problems, offer unique insights, or present information in a way that genuinely helps your readers. When you do this, you're not just establishing credibility—you're building trust. And in the world of business, trust is the most valuable currency of all.

So, how do you leverage this newfound credibility? Start by updating your professional profiles. Add "Author of [Your Book Title]" to your LinkedIn headline, your email signature, your business cards. When you speak at events or appear in media, make sure your book is mentioned. Your book is now part of your identity—wear it proudly.

### Your Book: The Ultimate Networking Superpower

Imagine walking into a networking event with a secret weapon—one that makes you instantly memorable, sparks fascinating conversations, and leaves people eager to connect with you further. That weapon is your book.

In a world where everyone has a elevator pitch, your book sets you apart. It's a conversation starter, a gift, and a demonstration of your expertise all rolled into one. When you meet someone interesting, don't just hand them a business card—give them your book. It's a gesture they'll remember, and it ensures that a piece of you stays with them long after the conversation ends.

But your book's networking power extends far beyond face-to-face interactions. It can open doors to partnerships, collaborations, and opportunities you might never have accessed otherwise. Influential people in your industry—the ones who seemed unreachable before—are now potential peers. After all, you're a published author now. You have something valuable to bring to the table.

Use your book to reach out to these influencers. Send them a copy with a personalized note, highlighting aspects of your work that align with their interests. Suggest collaboration opportunities or offer to contribute your expertise to their projects. Your book gives you the credibility to make these connections, and the content to make them meaningful.

Remember, networking isn't about collecting contacts—it's about building relationships. Your book is the foundation for those relationships, providing a depth of insight into who you are and what you offer that few other networking tools can match.

## Beyond Book Sales: Building Your Financial Empire

Let's be clear: selling books is great. There's something profoundly satisfying about seeing your royalty statements and knowing that people are buying your work. But if you're only focusing on book sales, you're leaving money on the table. Your book isn't just a product—it's the cornerstone of a much larger business strategy.

Think of your book as the hub of a wheel, with various revenue streams branching out like spokes. Each chapter, each key insight in your book, can be developed into a product or service. Did you write about leadership strategies? That could become a high-ticket executive coaching program. Is your book about personal finance? Consider creating an online course that walks people through implementing your strategies.

Here are just a few ways to monetize your expertise beyond book sales:

1. **Speaking Engagements**: Your book establishes you as an expert, making you an attractive speaker for conferences, corporate events, and workshops.

2. **Online Courses**: Develop in-depth courses that expand on the concepts in your book. These can provide passive income for years to come.

3. **Coaching and Consulting**: Offer one-on-one or group coaching sessions where you provide personalized guidance based on your book's principles.

4. **Membership Sites**: Create a community around your book's topic, offering ongoing support, resources, and exclusive content to members.

5. **Merchandise**: Develop products that complement your book—planners, workbooks, or even

branded items that reinforce your message.

**6. Licensing**: Allow companies or educational institutions to use your content in their training programs.

The key is to create a seamless ecosystem where each offering leads naturally to the next. Your book introduces people to your ideas. Those who resonate with your message might buy your online course. The most committed could then hire you for personalized coaching. It's a value ladder that allows you to serve—and profit from—readers at every level of engagement.

### Going Global: Your Book as a Passport to International Success

In today's interconnected world, there's no reason to limit your impact to a single country or language. Your book is your passport to global markets, allowing you to share your message and grow your business on an international scale.

Selling foreign rights is just the beginning. While seeing your book in different languages is thrilling, the real opportunity lies in using these international editions as launching pads for global business expansion. Each new market where your book appears is a new territory where you can offer speaking engagements, online courses, or consulting services.

But going global requires more than just translation. It demands cultural sensitivity and local market understanding. Your message may need to be adapted to resonate with different cultural contexts.

This isn't about changing your core ideas, but about presenting them in a way that connects with diverse audiences.

Consider partnering with local experts in your target markets. They can help you navigate cultural nuances, connect with local media, and tailor your offerings to meet specific market needs. Your book gives you the credibility to approach these potential partners, and together, you can create offerings that truly resonate in each new market.

Remember, expanding globally isn't just about reaching more people—it's about enriching your own understanding and broadening your perspective. The insights you gain from engaging with international audiences can fuel new ideas, leading to future books and business opportunities.

## The Content Ecosystem: Your Book as a Wellspring of Value

In the digital age, content is king. And guess what? Your book is a treasure trove of high-quality, carefully crafted content. But its value doesn't end once it's published. In fact, that's just the beginning.

Think of your book as a wellspring from which you can draw endless streams of content. Each chapter can become a series of blog posts. Key concepts can be turned into infographics or short videos. Memorable quotes can become social media posts. Your book provides a coherent framework for your ideas, and you can break this down into bite-sized pieces that keep your audience engaged across multiple platforms.

This approach serves several purposes:

1. It keeps your book's ideas fresh in people's minds long after they've finished reading.
2. It allows you to reach people who might not have read your book yet, drawing them into your world.
3. It positions you as a consistent source of valuable insights, reinforcing your expert status.
4. It provides multiple entry points to your value ladder, allowing people to engage with your ideas in the format they prefer.

But it's not just about repurposing existing content. Use your book as a springboard for new ideas. As you share your book's concepts, pay attention to the questions and comments you receive. These can inspire new content, helping you address your audience's evolving needs and interests.

By creating this content ecosystem, you ensure that your book continues to work for you long after its initial publication. It becomes a living, breathing part of your business strategy, constantly attracting new readers and opportunities.

### The Author's Mindset: From Writer to Entrepreneur

Here's a truth that many authors struggle with: writing a book is just the first step. To truly leverage your book for business growth, you need to shift your mindset from that of a writer to that of an entrepreneur.

This doesn't mean abandoning your love of writing or your commitment to sharing valuable ideas. Instead, it means approaching your book as a business asset—one that needs to be strategically positioned, marketed, and leveraged for growth.

Embrace the role of CEO of your own brand. Your book is your flagship product, but it's not your only offering. Think about your audience's needs and how you can serve them at different levels. Be proactive in seeking out opportunities to share your message. Don't wait for speaking invitations—reach out to event organizers and pitch yourself. Don't just hope for media coverage—build relationships with journalists and offer yourself as an expert source.

Most importantly, never stop learning and growing. The publication of your book isn't the end of your journey—it's a milestone on a much longer path. Stay curious. Keep refining your ideas. Be open to new opportunities and challenges. Your book has given you a platform—now it's up to you to build on it.

## Your Next Chapter Starts Now

As we close this guide, remember: your book is not the end of your journey. It's the beginning of a new chapter in your professional life—one filled with opportunities for growth, impact, and success. You've created something powerful. Now it's time to let it work for you.

Your words have the power to change lives, transform businesses, and open doors you never imagined. But that power is amplified when you approach your book not just as an author, but as a strategist, a brand builder, and an entrepreneur.

So, what's your next move? Will you develop that online course? Reach out to international partners? Launch a speaking career? The possibilities are endless, and the choice is yours. But whatever you decide, know that you don't have to navigate this journey alone.

At Ardith Publishing, we specialize in helping authors like you maximize the business potential of their books. Our team of experts can guide you through every step of the process, from developing your brand strategy to creating additional products and services based on your book.

Here's how you can take the next step in your author entrepreneurship journey:

1. **Sign up for the Ardith Publishing newsletter:** Get expert tips, proven strategies for leveraging your book, and insider knowledge delivered straight to your inbox. Our newsletter is your ongoing resource for turning your book into a thriving business.

2. **Contact Ardith Publishing:** Ready to transform your book into the cornerstone of a powerful personal brand? Our team of experienced publishing professionals is here to help. We'll work with you to develop a customized strategy that aligns with your book's message and your business goals.

Don't let your book's potential go unrealized. Your words have the power to build an empire—it's time to lay the foundation.

Contact Ardith Publishing today. Let's work together to turn your book into the launchpad for your business success. Your journey from author to entrepreneur is just beginning, and we're excited to be your guide on this transformative adventure.

Remember, in the world of business, your book is more than just a book—it's the beginning of your empire. Are you ready to reign?

mike@ardithpublishing.com
www.ardithpublishing.com

# Unlock the Real Power of Your Book:

## *Get the Workbook That Turns Pages into Profits*

Wrote a book but unsure what to do next? The *Pages to Profit Workbook* is your practical guide to turning that book into a business asset that brings in leads, clients, and authority. Whether you're a coach, consultant, or expert with a message, this workbook walks you step-by-step through building a strategy that actually uses your book to grow your business. From identifying your audience to setting up lead magnets, media outreach, content funnels, and premium offers—it's all here, clear and actionable.

Stop letting your book sit on a shelf (or in your hard drive). This isn't theory—it's a working tool to help you map out your content, position your authority, and build revenue streams around your message. Grab your free copy today and start putting your book to work in your business, where it belongs.

pages-to-profit-workbook-55934.getresponsesite.com